Prophets in Babylon

American University Studies

Series XXIV
American Literature
Vol. 28

PETER LANG
New York • San Francisco • Bern
Frankfurt am Main • Berlin • Wien • Paris

Margaret C. Jones

Prophets in Babylon

Five California Novelists in the 1930s

PETER LANG
New York • San Francisco • Bern
Frankfurt am Main • Berlin • Wien • Paris

Library of Congress Cataloging-in-Publication Data

Jones, Margaret C.
Prophets in Babylon: five California novelists in the 1930s / Margaret C. Jones.
p. cm. — (American university studies. Series XXIV, American literature; vol. 28)
Includes bibliographical references (p.).
1. American fiction—California—History and criticism.
2. American fiction—20th century—History and criticism.
3. California in literature. 4. Prophecies in literature. 5. Utopias in literature. I. Title. II. Series.
PS283.C2J6 1992 813'.520997794—dc20 91-32462
ISBN 0-8204-1750-5 CIP
ISSN 0895-0512

Die Deutsche Bibliothek-CIP-Einheitsaufnahme

Jones, Margaret C.:
Prophets in Babylon : five California novelists in the 1930s / Margaret C. Jones.—New York; Berlin, Bern; Frankfurt/M.; Paris; Wien; Lang, 1992
(American university studies; Ser. 24, American literature; Vol. 28)
ISBN 0-8204-1750-5
NE: American university studies/24

Contents

To my mother

Acknowledgements

I would particularly like to thank Professor Leonard Neufeldt, for his unflagging patience in reading and advising on successive drafts of this study of California novelists of the 1930s, and for a number of invaluable suggestions on the refinement and development of the original thesis.

I am also indebted to Professors Harold Woodman and Harry Targ for their helpful comments on matters related to the economic history and to the social protest literature of the period, to Professor Cheryl Oreovicz, for her thorough critical editing of the manuscript, and to the constructive criticism and advice of Professor Lester Cohen during the early stages of my research.

An unrepayable debt is due to the helpful librarians of the Eisenhower Library of Johns Hopkins University, of the library of Goucher College and of the State University of New York at Stony Brook (Donna Sammis, in the Inter-Library Loan office of the last-named institution, has a particularly heavy claim on my gratitude).

Finally, I wish to thank my husband, Essam Fattouh, for invaluable support and encouragement during the completion of this project under five different roofs, in four different states of the Union.

Preface

The American Dream, its ideology of unlimited individual opportunity, prosperity and empowerment, appears modified and intensified by historical context and geographic setting as the subject of a critique in the California fiction of the 1930s. As the most westerly outpost of European settlement on the North American mainland, California represented a final opportunity, historically and geographically speaking, to realize the promise of the American Dream, and, as one would expect, to do so in localized versions of the "California Dream." These versions of the California Dream, representing local variants of the American Dream, are organized by a number of images and motifs, particularly Hollywood, and a rural California as fertile Eden. During the Depression years, California's significance as gynaeceum and custodian of the American Dream was intensified by the acute economic and cultural contrasts within the state, between Hollywood's opulence and the desperate poverty of California's migrants. A further element important to an understanding of events in California during the Depression years is the state's tradition of utopian communities, and other utopian alternatives to the *status quo*.

Five novels set in the California of the 1930s offer a critique of the California Dream as a version of the American Dream. John Steinbeck's *The Grapes of Wrath*, Aldous Huxley's *After Many a Summer Dies the Swan*, Arnold B. Armstrong's *Parched Earth*, Nathanael West's *The Day of the Locust* and Upton Sinclair's *Co-op* each present a prophet-figure—moral teacher, visionary or sacrificial messiah—whose vision tends to contest and seeks to subvert a major feature of the California Dream rooted in competitive individualism. The prophet-figures reflect critically upon, and ultimately condemn, an ideology which justifies, indeed encourages, predatory greed. The figurative and literal correlatives of this ideology of the California Dream are deprivation, sterility, violence and death, whether in the fictional setting of a fruitful California valley, or in that of a Hollywood dream factory. (I use "ideology" to refer to a complex of collectively shared perceptions, interpretations, expressions sustaining of the existing social order. In no way is "ideology" regarded here as identical with "illusion.")

Alternatives to the assumptions and values of this California Dream and to the social behavior it sustains, are presented by most of the prophet-figures—by Steinbeck's Jim Casy, by Armstrong's Dave Washburn, by Huxley's William Propter and by Sinclair's reformers. Each of these prophet-figures preaches, in word and action, a utopia, in the Mannheimian sense. Their utopias involve the cultivation of a "state of mind" which, finding itself "incongruous" with the "state of reality" in which it occurs tends, therefore, to disrupt or shatter the *status quo*, the "order of things prevailing at the time" (*Ideology and Utopia* 85). In each case the utopia presented is one of cooperation, community, mutuality or solidarity, and entails an explicit critique of a reigning ideology of competitive individualism. All five critiques regard the latter as predatory and, in both individual and cultural terms, destructive.

This study is by no means the first to identify a utopian strain in California literature, or to consider utopian elements in relation to setting. Stoddard Martin has traced a utopian strain in his survey of fiction writers from Norris to Didion, *California Novelists* (1983). In *The Fall into Eden* (1986), David Wyatt has explored the question of the "appropriation" of California's natural space "for symbolic purposes" by nineteenth- and twentieth-century diarists, novelists and poets. The present study offers a rather different perspective on fiction written in and about California, in two respects. It concentrates on novels produced during a brief period of crisis, when the socioeconomic disparities and the utopian visions traditionally represented as characteristic of California society were fictionally depicted as having attained a peculiar intensity and centrality. The novels characteristic of the Depression decade in California arise out of, address the conditions of, and may even have assisted in shaping the perceptions of, their time and place. Secondly, this study seeks to explore the relationship between rural setting as a parody of Eden or Canaan, and its redemptive transformation through the explicit preaching of utopias of solidarity, community or mutuality by a variety of prophet-figures.

According to Mannheim, when in a given society the ascendance of a formerly subordinated class—and hence a shift in the prevailing ideology—seems to be a serious possibility, the "declassed intellectual" is likely to exhibit one of four possible reactions:

(i) alignment with the insurgent class

(ii) an effort to expose and destroy "ideological elements" in the science of the ascendant class, "in the name of intellectual integrity"

(iii) an escape into "spiritualization of the present" through appeal to an epoch or a society in which an "extinct form of reality transcendence" predominated

(iv) renunciation of participation in the historical process in favor of existentialism or apolitical mysticism. (254)

To many observers, U.S. society in the late 1930s appeared to be on the brink of just such a shift in class ascendance, and a corresponding response by intellectuals, as Mannheim alludes to. Indeed, the prophet-figures of the five novelists to be considered embrace three of the solutions outlined by Mannheim. Steinbeck's Jim Casy, and Armstrong's Communist labor leader, Dave Washburn, it will be argued, in varying degrees opt for the first response. West's Tod Hackett and Sinclair's utopian reformers incline more toward the second, and Huxley's mystic, William Propter, toward the fourth. The fictional prophets' visions may be regarded as concomitants of a specific historical moment when economic crisis opened broad possibilities for critique of certain destructive tendencies inherent in the prevailing ideology.

In presenting their critiques of the California Dream, Huxley, West, Steinbeck, Armstrong and Sinclair all make extensive use of parody. Parody functions in literary contexts as an alternative voice, and often as a "counter-voice," which questions the "primary voice" of a particular literary convention or conventions. Parody offers a new version alongside of, inviting comparison with, a familiar one. As a form of cooptation or appropriation, parody may entail both resistance to and accommodation to, the primary voice. It entails what Neufeldt has called "a transformation of convention as power," whereby the original convention may become, through its very appropriation in the form of parody, the source of the parody's effectiveness (161). Parody may expose a convention or conventions, but may also revitalize a convention by locating it in a new context.

The five Depression-era California novelists discussed in this study employ parody in all these ways. In particular, the novels appropriate and revitalize conventions by adapting them to the perceived demands of the socioeconomic and cultural crises of the 1930s. In their presentation of prophet-figures, the novels parody conventional types of religious or social leaders: Christ, Old Testament prophets, the gospel evangelist, the guru, the suffering artist, the labor organizer. A similar revitalization of convention through parody may be found in the novels' presentations of California as a parody of Eden and/or Canaan, in their use of female stereotypes, and in their presentation of Southern California as a parody of the New Jerusalem.

The visions of the five novelists' prophet-figures are products of, and potential influences upon, a society at a specific moment of economic and ideological crisis. At this moment, writers entertaining widely divergent utopian conceptions drew upon and appropriated California's rich traditions of cooperative experiment and of utopian "prophecy" to offer a variety of solutions. The present work represents a study of the novelists' manipulations of setting and character for the presentation of their social visions. It attempts to raise a further question: whether the type of setting represented (urban or rural) is conceived of as a factor in the success of the prophets' utopias; and finally, what the relevance of such a conception might be to a contemporary society faced with a different set of crises.

Chapter One

Babylon

To understand some of the critiques of the California Dream in California fiction of the 1930s it will be necessary briefly to glance at two tendencies—toward competitive individualism and toward utopian social cooperation respectively—which were already present in California in the nineteenth century.

Throughout the nineteenth century, pioneers and entrepreneurs carved their way westward across North America, fired by the idea of individual prosperity and empowerment in California's warm and fertile Eden. In the course of struggles over titles to land, water and minerals, a small number of individuals realized the California Dream in terms of a power and prosperity beyond their wildest expectations. Their opportunities came with the economic booms and ensuing cut-throat struggles over resources, typical not only of California but of other sectors of the North American frontier. The Gold Rush of the late 1840s and early 1850s, and the rise of great agricultural estates—wheat-growing in the 1860s, fruit-growing from the 1870s onward—made fortunes for a few. One of these few was Henry Miller, one-time tenant farmer, dispossessor of his former Spanish landlords, who through a monopoly of San Joaquin Valley water rights, by the end of the nineteenth century owned, in California and elsewhere, over a million acres.[1] Others were the founders of the Spreckels empire in sugar beets, or Leland Stanford, builder of railroads. One of their twentieth-century successors was Joseph di Giorgio, of the Di Giorgio Fruit Corporation, known in the late 1930s as the world's largest shipper of fresh fruit. In the wake of the landed millionaires came the tycoons of the newspaper and movie industries: William Randolph Hearst, who used his father's gift of the *San Francisco Examiner* to found a newspaper empire of his own; Harrison Gray Otis, turn-of-the-century owner of the *Los Angeles Times*; and the movie magnates, Carl Laemmle, Samuel Goldwyn, and Adolph Zukor. The enormous fortunes of these few individuals represent one result to which competitive pursuit of the California Dream might lead, in a minority of cases.

Yet there was an opposite tendency latent in the nineteenth-century version of the California Dream, a face which was to show itself again in California's politics and fiction of the 1930s. In the 1880s and 1890s the state became, for a few hundred settlers at most, a site for cooperative social experiments. California's welcoming climate, availability of land, and tolerant religious atmosphere, attracted those who believed in the North American Far West as the continent's last hope for the founding of utopias. These conditions attracted to California in turn, the religious colony of the heretic Swedenborgian Thomas Lake Harris, with his "Theo-Socialist" community at Fountain Grove (1875-1900); the Theosophists of Point Loma; and the French socialists of Icaria Speranza (1881-1886). Other utopian colonists were the Altrurians, Christian Socialist followers of William Dean Howells (whose 1894 experiment folded after a year), and the socialists at Kaweah, where the colony's founders included former San Francisco labor leaders Burnette Haskell and James Martin. Although economically successful, the Kaweah colony did not meet with the tolerance accorded other contemporary experiments in California. Its flourishing community was viewed as a threat by local timber magnates, who, after six years, used a legal technicality to have the colonists evicted from Kaweah (McWilliams, *Factories in the Field* 40-47).

According to Robert Hine in his study of *California's Utopian Colonies*, at least 17 groups attempted to found cooperative colonies in California from the 1880s to the early 1900s, a larger number than in any other state in the Union (6). This phenomenon continued after 1914 with the founding of the Socialist colony at Llano del Rio under the leadership of, among others, former Socialist candidate for mayor of Los Angeles, Job Harriman. Even after the colony's demise a number of former colonists were to lend their support to Upton Sinclair's cooperative EPIC program when he ran for governor of California in 1934, thus creating a link between the tradition of the cooperative colonies and the utopian aspirations of the 1930s (Hine 177).

By the early twentieth century there seemed little doubt, however, as to which system of social organization would prevail. With the socialist colony a marginalized utopia, and with particular economic developments, including the outbreak of World War I and the wave of anti-radical sentiment that accompanied and followed it, it was clear that in the foreseeable future the shaping of California's development was in the hands of California's entrepreneurs and corporations. For them, the second decade of the twentieth century was, as elsewhere in the United States, a particularly propitious time. Wartime demand had stimulated production. The oil industry greatly expanded, with production rising from one hundred million barrels a year in 1920 to 227 million in 1930 (Roske 486). California agriculture continued to expand during the 1920s and 1930s, so that by 1937 the state's total crop was valued at $648,200,000, making the state the nation's leader in agricultural production (484-89). Pioneering work had begun in movie making at the turn of the century. As early as 1923, movie companies accounted for one-fifth of the state's annual manufacturing production (495). During this period, moreover, California's population grew from under 3,500,000 to 5,600,000 within ten years. (By 1940 it had reached nearly seven million [Caughey 430].) Los Angeles alone saw a growth of 114 per cent within two decades.

Carey McWilliams, California historian and one-time Commissioner for Immigration and Housing, has commented on this astonishingly rapid growth as it appeared to him as a newcomer to California in the 1920s. The "storybook version of the American Dream," as McWilliams calls the westward expansion into California, was, in his words,

> given its penultimate stage in a semi-tropical setting at the western edge of the continent. . . . The various phases of economic development—pastoral, agricultural, "cottage industries," industrialization . . . came in such rapid succession that the region's growth seemed staged or contrived, like an outdoor pageant or a motion picture being shot on location. (*The Education* 42)

The motion picture image is an apt one. Kevin Starr, in *Inventing the Dream*, has pointed to the interpenetration, in the California setting, of the movie dream world and the pre-existing image of

California as a Western Eden. He cites as an example D. W. Griffith's *The Thread of Destiny*, a romantic tale of Old California, filmed in 1910 at the eighteenth-century California mission of San Gabriel. As Starr notes, the film "linked Southern California and film together at a common point of symbolic beginning" (292). The idealized setting evoked by the Griffith film endorsed the image of California as the Garden.

If Hollywood fed on older images of the California setting, it also generated its own images. Griffith's legendary cinematic version of Babylon in the 1916 film *Intolerance* is a case in point. The film included a celebrated Belshazzar's Feast scene in which hundreds of dancers on a 300-foot high set of elaborate temple statuary evoked the splendors of the doomed city (Starr 304-5). This scene not only inspired a spate of later Biblical epics, but created an image of Hollywood as implicitly a version of Babylon which Nathanael West, in *The Day of the Locust*, would employ for his own literary purposes. Hollywood, like California's fertile valleys, became one more setting onto which the California Dream might be projected—and for the disillusioned provided an image of all that was undesirable in the competitive individualism that sustained it.

The "Babylon" of Hollywood is to be understood, then, as an aspect of the interpenetration of California dream and popular movie illusion; and for Nathanael West a metaphor for American society. A fellow-screen-writer-novelist of West's puts the point more explicitly. In Budd Schulberg's words,

> All the values of American society, the good ones and the false ones, are to be found in Hollywood, not realistically reflected but grotesquely magnified . . . . the Hollywood of Monroe Starr and the last tycoons—was like one of those distortion mirrors in amusement parks where a child is transformed into a giant and a forefinger becomes the Tower of Pisa. ("Writers in America" 21)

In such caricaturing terms Hollywood registered and invoked the American Dream, and the California version of it, for the nation. On their opulent estates its stars lived private lives "that were also public performances."[2] They presented the public with an American version of aristocracy in which, unlike the titled families of Europe, they existed to promote the idea of progress for the individual from obscure beginnings to fame, wealth and influence. A Dorothy Lamour might rise from department store elevator operator to a pinnacle of goddess-like celebrity, becoming a star whom the third largest crowd in Detroit's history would turn out to see (Rosten 11, 14). By implication such an opportunity was open to every aspirant from a similarly humble background. It was only necessary to move West—to golden California, to Hollywood.

Ironically, the social and economic hierarchy of 1930s Hollywood presented notable disparities which, as in American society at large, somewhat called into question the promise of equal and unlimited opportunity. It has been estimated that two-thirds of Hollywood's extras, for instance, annually earned less than $500—a full $280 below California's poverty line (Balio 276).

If film extras and low-paid Hollywood workers had reason to complain of their lot, by the late 1930s there was abundant material to feed a critique of the California Dream in the world outside Hollywood's gates. The desperate economic situation of many Californians and migrants to California could make the grievances of Hollywood employees seem trivial. Per capita income in the state from 1929 to 1938 fell 29 per cent. By 1934 more than one and a quarter million Californians—about one-fifth of the state's population—found themselves on relief (Bean 409). In 1939 the San Diego coroner's reports attributed nearly one-third of all San Diego suicides, which had recently shown a significant increase, to economic causes (Wilson, *American Earthquake* 419). The crisis was particularly grave for the migrant workers in California's fields and orchards. Although migration into California in the 1930s fell to 40 per cent of what it had been in the previous decade, from 1935 to 1939 some 285,000 new, largely destitute migrants, "Okies" and "Arkies" from the Dust Bowl, found themselves competing for the already ill-paid jobs of Mexican and Filipino migrants, in what Carey McWilliams has called the "factories in the field." Although their arrival created a panic among California residents about additions to the already swollen welfare rolls, it benefitted the farm employer by pushing down the average agricultural worker's wage.

No doubt many of the 1930s migrants came to "the land of sunshine and oranges," as Nathanael West's narrator dubs California in *The Day of the Locust*, not only out of a sense of despair over conditions in the old home, but also out of an unshakeable faith in the California Dream. California was for them, in the words of John Caughey, "a special asylum. . . . They were attracted by the mildness of the climate which made it seem a better place in which to endure privation, and they were lured by the state's traditional aura as a land of promise and opportunity" (454).

Ironically, then, in the feverish political climate of the Depression era, the California Dream seems to have taken on an even more sensational and compelling aspect than in earlier years—and to have changed its sign, as it were, and acquired something of a utopian coloring for migrants to California. According to the *Oakland Tribune* of August 2, 1935, "Some of the Dust Bowl refugees had heard . . . that Upton Sinclair was running the state and abolishing poverty. Others thought that Huey Long had started his share-the-wealth scheme in California" (Stein 81). "This country is the promised land," a Dust Bowl migrant to California reportedly told a *New York Times* reporter in 1937. He had made "$240 cash money" in a season's work ("Exiles" 1).

On an average annual family income of $350-400 in 1930, dropping to $289 in 1935 (the year in which the California State Relief Administration drew the poverty line at $780) most of these migrants were sorely disillusioned. Many, according to Richard Nebberger, writing in 1939 for the *Survey Graphic*, were employed under conditions in which malnutrition might be regarded as "an occupational disease" (520). At the same time, of 157 farms surveyed in 1935 by the California State Relief Administration, every one reported a profit.

As public criticism of the migrants' conditions mounted, fueled by, among other forces, the San Joaquin Valley famine of 1937, the violent breaking of migrant strikes in earlier years, and the writings of Carey McWilliams, Richard Nebberger and John Steinbeck, the migrants' employers felt obliged to defend themselves against charges of exploitation and of denial of their employees' First Amendment rights. Publicly, at least, many viewed the migrants' lot as a contented one, and would have subscribed to the version of the migrant life given by a grower several decades earlier: "The pickers sing and play banjos and they make love and gossip—and turn in at all hours of the night, always good-natured and jolly and carefree" (McWilliams, *Factories* 174). According to George Thomas Miron, hired by the Associated Farmers in 1939 to write

The Truth About John Steinbeck and the Migrants, the typical "bosses, foremen, crop contractors and farmers" of California were, moreover, "a very considerate group of men, well-liked by the workers generally." Miron maintains, on the one hand, that the majority of migrants he came across in California "were receiving more money per day than they ever had before in their entire lives," and, on the other, that "much of the suffering" of the workers was due to their own inexperience with California farm work. His assessment is supplemented by, possibly grounded in, a version of social Darwinism characteristically employed by apologists for predatory individualism. "Like anywhere else in American life of course," Miron writes, "it was always very apparent that the enterprising, the ambitious, the energetic, the higher grade citizens were making their way," while "the other kind were not doing so well" (21-22). The picture painted by Ruth Comfort Mitchell, wife of conservative Republican state senator Colonel Sanborn Young, in her 1940 novel *Of Human Kindness*, was likewise one in which the vast majority of California growers were humane employers, offering the migrant workers "fair wages," with "decent cabins and . . . clean water and shower baths and shade trees" (40). The migrants' sufferings, in Mitchell's version, were all traceable to their own ignorance, which the "awakened social conscience" of the landowners would eventually cure with "California common sense and humanity" (91, 178). Woody Guthrie's ballad for the migrant workers, however, offers a very different view:

> California's a Garden Of Eden
> A paradise to live in or to see . . .
> But believe it or not
> You won't find it so hot
> If you ain't got the Do Re Mi.

Some landowners were quite frank about the conditions of migrant farm labor in California. In 1920, a full fifteen years before the arrival of the Dust Bowlers, one grower described how his employees camped in tents by the roadside and drew their drinking water from stagnant puddles in a dried-up creek bed (McWilliams, *Factories* 197). Another, when interviewed in 1939, was equally frank about his intention to prevent workers from organizing to improve their conditions. The secretary of the Imperial Valley Associated Farmers, asked by a member of the La Follette Committee investigating "union-busting" in California whether he regarded the formation of an agricultural labor union as ever justified replied, "Not to the point where the farmer loses control of the workers" (Auerbach 189).

A concomitant of efforts by a number of landowners to present the agricultural employer in a favorable light was the portrayal of such employers primarily as small farmers. The struggling farm widow in *Of Human Kindness* is a Ma Joad figure, "Old Buddha in a faded gingham dress," whose fellow farm wives take in washing to make ends meet. The Associated Farmers, the main organization representing growers in Southern and Central California from 1934 onwards, presented itself to possible members as an association of "your neighbors . . . banded together in order to grow your crops . . . and transport them to market, under the rights guaranteed by the American form of government" (3-4).[3] Yet the majority of California migrant workers were not employees of Ma Joad, or of some "perspiring toiler with a rugged countenance" (Nebberger 518) but of enterprises like Joseph di Giorgio's California Packing Corporation, which during the summer season employed annually 35,000 people. Some two percent of the landowners owned 25 per cent of total California farm acreage (Nebberger 520). Ten per cent of all farmers between 1930 and 1940 produced roughly one half of California's agricultural output (Cleland 375). Over forty per cent of Associated Farmers funding came not from farmers at all, but from large banks, and utility, railroad and packing companies, including the Southern Pacific Railroad, the Pacific Gas and Electric Company, the Canners' League and the San Joaquin Cotton Oil Company (Chambers 45). It was the organized power of California's most successful entrepreneurs and corporations which, through the Associated Farmers, strove to combat the attacks of "radical and subversive" elements that, according to A. F. spokesman George Miron, only wished to stir up class strife. "I can think of no other novel," Miron wrote, "which advances the idea of class war—in the most classless society in the world—more than does 'The Grapes of Wrath'" (7).

Miron's accusation seems to be a classic case of blaming the messenger for ill news. Although California growers during the

1930s employed no more than five per cent of all U.S. farm labor, the state became notorious for the frequency of its agricultural strikes. Thirty-four of them involved more than one thousand workers, and the estimated 140 strikes throughout the decade involved 127,000 people in all. In the San Joaquin Valley cotton strike of 1933 at least fifteen thousand workers struck, shutting down the region's cotton industry for twenty-four days. Jerrold Auerbach scarcely exaggerates when he asserts that California's agricultural valleys during the decade were at times in a condition verging on armed class warfare (177). From the abortive organizing efforts of ethnic unions in the early 1930s, through those of the Communist-led Cannery and Agricultural Workers Industrial Union in 1933-34, to 1937 when the Communists joined the newly-founded United Cannery, Agricultural, Packing and Allied Workers of America, California strikes had been remarkable for their number and intensity, and for the degree of violence brought against workers. The Associated Farmers mobilized vigilantes to break up labor protests with clubs, guns and tear gas. In the Salinas lettuce strike the husband of Ruth Comfort Mitchell, Colonel Sanborn Young, took over the functions of County Sheriff and Salinas Chief of Police and drafted 2500 deputies to break the strike. Of this conflict—"L'Affaire Lettuceberg," as Steinbeck was later to refer to it in connection with a projected satirical novel—he wrote to a friend, "There are riots in Salinas and killings in the streets of that dear little town where I was born. I shouldn't wonder if the thing had begun. I don't mean any general revolt but an active beginning aimed toward it" (*Letters* 132).

As one might expect, a crisis of the intensity of California's landowner-migrant conflict, given its context, spawned a number of utopias and prophet-figures, some of them in unexpected places. The Federal government was one such unexpected agency for the dissemination of utopian thought. Admittedly, its somewhat half-hearted establishment of fifteen model camps for migrants was dismissed by one *New York Times* reporter as a "drop in the bucket."[4] (This measure was also open to the criticism that it merely offered a readily available supply of cheap labor to the landowner without doing anything permanently to alter working conditions.) Nonetheless, the camps proved a *de facto* haven for workers' organizations. Five camps had their own Workers'

Alliance or UCAPAWA locals, and all permitted on-site CIO organizing. Many of the camp managers appointed by the federal government, like Milan Dempster, the socialist manager at Marysville, actively promoted such union work (Stein 252).

Another experiment with a potentially utopian aspect to emerge from the federal government's intervention in the affairs of the migrants was the establishment of a cooperative farm at Mineral King Farm, near Visalia. Sixty-six families were settled on the cooperatively owned farm directed by a government-employed manager who assigned tasks and set prices for marketing of produce. The farm's ultimate aim, in accordance with New Deal capitalist ideology, was to return each of the cooperative's members in time to individual economic self-sufficiency, rather than to perpetuate the cooperative model. Indeed, in 1943 the families at Mineral King disbanded the cooperative and shared out the farm's profits among themselves (Stein 160). The idea of cooperative farming seems to have appealed more to the middle-class idealists who formulated the plan than it did to the Okies, "country businessmen" as they have been called (Stein 265). But the experiment had given a demonstration of successful cooperative enterprise to California society as a whole. The success of Mineral King offered a practical example of Carey McWilliams' dreams of "a new type of agricultural economy" for the West and for America (*Factories* 325).

If a capitalist state, perceiving an imminent threat of class war, could through national policies foster collective experiments, it is not surprising that workers' organizations, urban and rural, brought forth labor leaders, labor heroes and preachers of collective solidarity of their own. The tradition of labor heroes and labor prophets in California was by 1929 already an established one. The state could claim association with Joe Hill, who had spent several years in California in the 1900s, and with the Wobbly heroes of the "free speech fights" in Fresno and San Diego in 1910 and 1912. More recently prominent figures were Tom Mooney, jailed from 1916-1938 on a trumped-up murder charge and pardoned by the newly-elected Governor Olson in that year, and Pat Chambers and Carolyn Decker, whose organizing work for the CAWIU came to an abrupt end in 1934 when they were jailed under California's criminal syndicalism law.

In folk-singer Woody Guthrie, who sang on Los Angeles radio station KFVD and performed for labor groups and in migrant camps as a self-dubbed "prophet-singer," the migrant agricultural workers found another labor prophet to describe their conditions and express their grievances. Guthrie's ballad "Tom Joad," which faithfully traces the narrative outline of *The Grapes of Wrath*, was written after Guthrie saw the Ford/Johnson film version of Steinbeck's novel. Guthrie explained: "The people back in Oklahoma haven't got two bucks to buy the book, or even thirty cents to see the movie, but the song will get back to them and tell them what Preacher Casy said" (Greenway 289).

The final two stanzas of Guthrie's ballad paraphrase Jim Casy's words about the world being composed of "one big soul." They conclude with Tom Joad's statement about communion with humanity after death: "Wherever they's a fight so hungry people can eat, I'll be there." Yet they give it a slightly more militant emphasis:

> Wherever little children are hungry and crying,
> Wherever people ain't free
> Wherever men are fighting for their rights
> That's where I'm a-gonna be. (Greenway 291)

California labor leaders in the field needed the militancy of Guthrie's Joad to sustain them. They also seem at times to have shared some of the characteristics of Steinbeck's Jim Casy; for among the most successful organizers of the Dust Bowl migrants, with their conservative suspicion of anything that smacked of "communism," were those leaders who combined their union gospel with a theological one. These labor leaders, Baptists and Pentecostalists, preached a curious blend of "religion and strike propaganda" (Stein 268). This involvement of religious leaders in labor organizing seems to have predated the arrival of the Okies. During the 1933 San Joaquin cotton strike, primarily involving Mexican workers, a local minister carrying a Bible, a union card, and a Communist Party card, rallied the strikers with the cry, "By the aid of God and a strong picket line" (McWilliams, *Factories* 221).

In the fiction of the period, the labor leader becomes a prophet for both John Steinbeck and for Arnold Armstrong, whose Dave

Washburn in his own person links the older IWW tradition to that of the Communist organizers of the 1930s. Although the closest counterparts of Jim Casy and Dave Washburn may be found in the rural setting of the harvest field, those of Huxley's William Propter—as well as some examples of communitarian, utopian ideals—must be sought for in the urban setting. As with the labor preachers of the migrants, a blending of the theological with the socioeconomic was a not uncommon feature of the urban prophet's messages.

Los Angeles was a particularly fertile ground for the dissemination of such messages, as it had been for decades. By the 1920s the city was famous for its cultists, preachers, yogis and its extraordinary range of religious sects. Carey McWilliams estimates that in 1926 Los Angeles had seven distinctly separate "churches" of the American Theosophical Association and 29 affiliates of the National Spiritualist Association. He found it impossible, he writes, "to keep track" of the growth of lesser-known "cults, occult sciences and religions" (*Education* 46-47). These would have included "Fire-brands for Jesus," the Psychosomatic Institute, and "Nothing Impossible" (Roske 496).

Among Christian sects, probably the most famous were those of the Reverend Robert Shuler and of Aimee Semple McPherson, fierce rivals for the souls and pocketbooks of the citizens of Los Angeles. While Shuler's appeal was that of a traditional fire-and-brimstone fundamentalist—coupled with a talent for rooting out and publicizing sensational scandals among the city's public figures, a gift through which he acquired substantial influence over Los Angeles city government—McPherson preached a gospel of divine mercy and love, enlivened by music, spectacle and drama. Although her celebrity value to the press had begun to wane somewhat by the end of the 1930s, she remained a powerful influence on her California followers.

Unorthodox religions in California often gave a religious cast to non-religious political movements. A number of the Temple Home faction of the Theosophists, for instance, voiced their support in the 1900s for the Socialist Party.[5] Conversely, non-religious political or social reform movements sometimes adopted the rituals and ceremonies more commonly associated with organized religion. The Utopian Society is a case in point. An offshoot of the Technocracy Movement which flourished in California in the early 1930s (calling for a government of technocrats who would abolish the profit system), the Utopian Society promoted a similar variety of state socialism. Much of its popular appeal, however, seems to have been attributable to those features which distinguished it from Technocracy. According to Carey McWilliams, the Society's success was due partly to the "secret" or "fraternal" mode of organization in which initiates "kept repeating a vow of secrecy as they moved to a new cycle." McWilliams took an observer's interest in these sessions, which, for all their allegedly clandestine nature, were apparently open to gate-crashing by the uninitiated. Sitting in on the Society's rites, McWilliams found them to be a dramatic representation of "mankind's quest for abundance" in six cycles—a "series of revelations as in a Biblical play or parable" (*Education* 68). By the summer of 1934, the Utopian Society could claim an initiated membership of half a million. A single rally of the Society in June, in the Hollywood Bowl, was attended by 25,000 people.

Even so apparently nonreligious a movement as that of the Townsend Clubs—which Jay Martin identifies as one of those groups which gave Nathanael West "a hint of the economic frustration of the Torch-bearers" in *The Day of the Locust*—took on a religious tinge, when some of the clubs' members began referring to the movement's founder as a "Christ reincarnate" (307). The Townsend Clubs, and the Old Age Revolving Pensions plan they existed to promote, were the brainchild of a retired physician, Francis E. Townsend. The movement began with his letter to the Long Beach Press in September 1933 in which Townsend proposed his scheme whereby every Californian would be retired at the age of sixty on a pension of $150 a month (later raised to $200). The following year the plan was incorporated as Old-Age Revolving Pensions Ltd.; and by November 1934 there were already 1200 Townsend Clubs in California, with the movement spreading beyond the state's borders.

The efforts of "Christ reincarnate" and his followers petered out when the Roosevelt Administration passed the Social Security act in 1935, but not before they had given birth to the "Ham-'n-Eggs" scheme of Robert Noble, a radio show host on Los Angeles Station KMTR. Ham-'n-Eggs was a plan to give every elderly person a weekly allowance to be spent within an allotted time, thereby, it was claimed, restimulating the stagnant economy by promoting consumer spending. Pirated by Willis and Lawrence Allen, the plan, which at the height of its popularity had 360,000 active supporters, was actually submitted to a statewide referendum vote in 1934 and narrowly defeated, 1,398,999 to 1,143,670. In 1939 it was defeated by a wider margin, of nearly one million votes (Burke 33, 112).

If the Townsend and Ham-'n-Eggs movements seemed to take on some of the fervor of a moral crusade, Upton Sinclair's bid for the governorship on the Democratic ticket and the campaign slogan "End Poverty in California" as conceived and largely directed by a pious socialist with a powerful gift of self-dramatization, became a prophetic mission, with the prophet playing his center-stage role to the hilt.

Sinclair's EPIC plan, as expounded in his campaign pamphlet, *I, Governor of California and How I Ended Poverty in California*, proposed the setting up by the state government of agricultural and industrial cooperatives based on a system of "production for use" under qualified management, where workers would be paid in scrip valid as currency within the cooperative system. He also proposed a progressive state income tax and inheritance tax, and a number of social security and welfare measures.

Sinclair saw his proposal for agricultural cooperatives in particular as a third alternative to the evils of small-scale farming, in which farmers found themselves "in bondage to the banks," or to California's large-scale corporation-owned enterprises, which employed migrant laborers under "what amounts to peonage" (14). Attacking that "little band of insiders" in control of the state's industries and agriculture, Sinclair ascribed to them "the mentality of birds of prey" (6). In the imaginary scenario of his campaign for governor outlined in *I, Governor*, he portrays himself rejecting the NIRA symbol of the blue eagle because of its predatory connotations, in favor of the industrious, cooperative bee (9). He depicts himself as governor, addressing the members of EPIC's first cooperative colony. "It is up to you," the governor tells them, "to prove that human beings do not have to be prowling wolves or sly lynxes, but can be rational, just, and kindly members of a commonwealth" (55).

Sinclair further describes in quasi-religious terms his personal sense of mission to preach the cooperative message. A part of his mind, he writes, which assumes the form of "the voice which wakes me in the middle of the night" tells him, "What the people need is somebody they can trust—who will show them the way, who will lift a banner and call them to follow it" (5).

Not only in this printed manifesto, but in his campaign as a whole, Sinclair seems to have promoted the image of himself as a religious prophet and cultural savior. Five years later he was to liken *The Grapes of Wrath* to his own novel *The Jungle* as a shining example of the socialist evangel: "I remember how Elijah put his mantle on the shoulders of Elisha. John Steinbeck can have my old mantle if he has any use for it" (Stein 203). As Carey McWilliams wrote in a 1934 article for the *Baltimore Sun*, Sinclair did not hesitate to proclaim that "he is representing the Lord Jesus Christ in California politics, and that he will end poverty not only in California but in civilization" ("Party Lines" 2).

In McWilliams' judgement the candidate's assumption of the prophetic mantle was not wholly disingenuous, for Sinclair's Republican opponent, Frank Merriam, was eager to "pin the atheistic label" upon him ("Tide Swinging" 21). Sinclair, an "accomplished theologian and expert in piety," who grew ever "more fervently Christian" as the campaign progressed, had, in McWilliams' words, "Skillfully stolen the show." Attacked by right-wing clergymen, including Father Coughlin, Sinclair was endorsed by a number of liberal church leaders in California and elsewhere. The Rev. John Hughes Holmes of New York hailed him as a "modern prophet" (the words "prophet," "prophecies" and "prophetic" appear four times in Holmes' two-page statement) whose past "prophecies" of the development of capitalism have been fulfilled, who writes with "prophetic" fire. Sinclair is "a prophet justified in his own time by the course of events" (Introduction to *I, Governor* 64).

By Fall 1934 two thousand EPIC clubs supported Sinclair's bid for the California governorship. A Republican campaign, however, made unscrupulous use of bogus newsreels and fake stories to imply that Sinclair's campaign was already bringing thousands of destitute immigrants to California from other parts of the United States (Swanberg 448). Moreover, a split in traditional Democrat support between Sinclair's candidacy and that of Raymond Haight (Progressive, Republican, and Commonwealth) left Merriam victorious with 48.8% of the vote. Sinclair gathered 37.3%. More than two million votes altogether were cast in support of EPIC.

The vote, like the wide popularity of the Townsend Plan and of the Utopian Society, indicates the extent to which California's citizens were willing to entertain the idea of utopian alternatives—which often, as in Sinclair's proposals, opposed an ideal of cooperation to a harshly competitive individualism they characterized as predatory. Three movements—of the Utopian Society, of the Townsendites and of EPIC—also exemplify the degree to which it was possible for bewildered victims of the Depression and for would-be deliverers, to imbue socioeconomic concerns with religious connotations, and to make of the would-be social savior a holy prophet.

The fiction writers of the period invoke a powerful cultural convention in creating prophet-figures who are also saviors. What indeed could be more compelling to the writer, given the confusion of the times and the diversity of the self-declared prophets of utopia, than the urge to present to the public an attractive literary protagonist who might somehow help to open the eyes of the ideologically blind to the hope beyond the contemporary chaos, of a newer, better world? Writers like Steinbeck, Huxley, Armstrong, and even West (whose prophet preaches no utopia) attempt to engage the complex of assumptions, values and behavior in the system within which they market their texts, to see their texts as agents as well as effects of sociocultural change.[6] The context in which the fictional prophet-figures created for these purposes operate, and the nature and viability of the prophets' messages, will be the subject of the chapters which follow.

Notes

1 McWilliams, *Factories in the Fields* 38.

2 Starr, *Inventing the Dream* 335.

3 "Who Are the Associated Farmers?" *The Associated Farmer* 15 April 1940: 3-4.

4 Todd, 11.

5 "All Theosophists should be socialists," one member said.

6 It should be borne in mind that the "California" of the 1930s novels to be studied exists (to borrow a phrase from Terry Eagleton's *Criticism and Ideology*) as the "product of a representational process" that signifies not California *per se*, but a particular ideological or utopian experience of the "historical" California of 1929-1941. The composite picture given in this chapter represents an attempt to foreground those elements of California society which seem to have most affinity with the fictional prophets' denunciations, and also those utopian elements in the social thought of Californians which find a fictional parallel in the prophets' messages of William Propter, Jim Casy and Dave Washburn, and of Sinclair's prophet-figures in *Co-op*.

Chapter Two

Pastures of Plenty

California novelists present the state as a parody of Eden or of Canaan, and sometimes as both, holding forth to those who come in quest of it a deceptive promise of abundance.[1]

(The term "parody" is used here, as elsewhere in these chapters, to denote a "counter-voice" that challenges and questions the voice of the original; but is also used in this chapter in the more restricted sense of a mocking, ironic travesty). In *Parched Earth*, *The Grapes of Wrath*, *After Many a Summer* and *Co-op*, California is presented as failing to live up to the expectations of the questing migrants. It reveals itself as a land of deprivation in the midst of plenty, offering a parodic contrast with the original ideas of Eden or Canaan—of a lush garden, or a land of milk and honey. The four novels appropriate these conventional images to demonstrate the contrast between the migrants' dreams of California and the actual conditions they encounter.[2]

Out of disillusionment with this promise of individual self-fulfillment a utopia of community, or of communal mutual support within the context of the rural/agricultural setting becomes an alternative. Prophet-figures in *Parched Earth*, *The Grapes of Wrath*, *After Many a Summer* and *Co-op* preach a marxist-leninist utopia, a utopia of community and mutual support, a philosophic-anarchist utopia and a cooperative socialist utopia respectively. "Utopian," as it describes the messages of the prophet-figures in these novels does not, of course, imply that the messages are false or illusory. "Utopian" is used in the present context to denote a complex of ideas or ideals at least potentially realizable at a future date. The utopias are presented in each case as viable alternatives, firstly, because the potential converts of the prophet-figures in the novels are deracinated and destitute and, secondly, because the prophets point the way to a social/political condition in which a utopia of community will have established itself. A further issue in the development of the utopia in each novel, however, and directly linked to the viability of the utopian program, is the question of control of technology—specifically of forms of ownership of the machine in California's garden.

The four novels share in common depiction of the rural/agricultural setting as a parody of Eden or Canaan; growth of characters' realization that California is *not* the Promised Land, providing a context for the growth of communally oriented and/or cooperative behavior in a rural/agricultural setting. Furthermore, the novels display a common interest in the social role of technology and the question of its ownership.

Parched Earth is the earliest of the four to be published. It draws its prophet-figure from the tradition of the proletarian novel upon which, as Granville Hicks correctly perceived, *The Grapes of Wrath* also draws.[3] In *Parched Earth*, however, the fruitful agrarian setting, and the disillusionment it engenders for those excluded from sharing its abundance—above all, the figure of the social prophet—are merely sketched in. In *The Grapes of Wrath* they are developed with much greater detail and somewhat more subtlety, albeit to serve a different utopian ideal from that of *Parched Earth*. *After Many A Summer* and *Co-op* present the agrarian setting and the prophet-figure's role in it differently from *Parched Earth* or *The Grapes of Wrath*. While these two novels deal with labor conflict and present their prophet-figures as strike leaders, *After Many a Summer* and *Co-op* celebrate the achievement of harmony by a few people dwelling on a society's margins, in small communities, which may offer an experimental example. Dealing with Huxley's and Sinclair's novels after Armstrong's and Steinbeck's offers scope for extended discussion of this basic distinction.

Before addressing the ways in which the four novels differ, however, it will be necessary to consider those features which they share. Perhaps the most important, since it makes the presentation of the prophet-figures and their utopias possible in the first place, is presentation of the agrarian setting as a Promised Land. "This is blossom time in Tontos Valley, and folks back in the cold bitter East just plain envy us lucky Californians. Brr - yessir!" (*Parched Earth* 32). The radio announcer who thus heralds the spring and the approach of the town's annual Fiesta, "Under the sponsorship of local merchants" in *Parched Earth*, broadcasts to California listeners a message essentially akin to that heard through other channels by the migrants. California is not only imagined to be a land of abundance and warmth when contrasted with the "bitter" East, but also one of human liberality, fellowship, shared production and shared rewards.

It is this dream of free access to the state's natural abundance that in *Parched Earth*, as in *The Grapes of Wrath*, Huxley's *After Many a Summer* and *Co-op*, draws the migrant workers: "Leaky, wheezing Fords, carrying whole families . . . rumble along the asphalt roads. Hitch-hikers . . . cast glances at the golden fruit which hangs on branches awaiting pails and hands" (141). In *The Grapes of Wrath* the golden fruit is imagined from afar as being even more accessible for unrestricted consumption: "Jus' let me go to California where I can pick me an orange when I want it" (90). As they journey the Joads dream aloud of pictures seen on calendars of white houses among orchards (163), of "everything nice an' green, an' little white houses an' oranges growin' aroun'" (119). In *After Many a Summer* the migrants come to California "as to a promised land" (94). In general, the migrants enter California in a state of unawareness—or like the Joads, unbelieving of what they have been told—that the promised land of California, although "a nice country," was "stole a long time ago" (225). In *The Grapes of Wrath* a similar note of free access to abundance is sounded: "They don't care how much you eat 'cause they got so much" (161).[4]

In *The Grapes of Wrath* rural landscape becomes an image of moral and social ambiguity, as new arrivals to California strive to make sense of their situation. The image of water mirages on Route 66 in Chapter Twelve (132) points forward to the Joads' first sight of California—not a garden but a desert, in which Granma Joad will die before reaching the green land. "This here *is* California," Tom Joad tells his father as they stare at the bare mountainous country before the crossing. There is green land too, of course, but even the green country is fraught with deception. The river by the willows where the Joad family rest before the crossing lures Noah Joad away from the group (229). As the family finally enter the green country they see its richness—and among the green, orange and gold of the valley landscape a windmill, its blades flashing "like a little heliograph," but whose message is indecipherable by the Joads (251). As they descend into the valley a rattlesnake crosses their path (253). Not only the serpent in the garden, but even the "twisting and looping" of the valley road suggests a labyrinth of perceptions that can confuse and deceive the Joads as they pursue the mirage of their Promised Land. As they enter California their paeon of praise for the state's abundance is interrupted by a sourer note: "You go in there an' plant you a little corn, an' you'll go to jail!" (225).

In *Co-op*, the Jett family, migrants evicted from rented land in Louisiana, arrive in California "in a state of exaltation" which "blinds" them to "reality." The sunshine seems to them "more dazzling, the flowers gayer," than in the places they have left (101). Cristy Jett even worries about defiling the sacred soil of California by bringing in his tick-infested dog, to which his more practical wife suggests, "Doan' you reckon they got 'em here?" (98).

In all four novels the characters who entertained visions of California as a Promised Land, or as Eden, quickly become disillusioned by their experiences in the Golden State—above all by their realization that deprivation and destitution are, ironically, quite compatible with natural abundance. In *Parched Earth* the small farmer Abe Jenkins destroys the rows of peach trees that can bring him no commercial profit owing to the fixing of fruit prices over which he, unlike the local tycoon Everett Caldwell, has no control. Although from a commercial point of view he is judged to be "raisin' too much fruit," there are, he points out, "folks in cities who never tasted an apricot" (371-72). In *The Grapes of Wrath* Tom Joad expresses what the rest of his family have discovered but do not explicitly voice: "This ain't no lan' of milk an' honey like the preachers say. They's a mean thing here" (276). In *After Many a Summer* the novel's representative migrant, the man from Kansas, reflects bitterly upon his situation: "Only half a day, the man was thinking. . . . They'd be lucky if they made as much as seventy-five cents . . . and the right front tyre wasn't going to last much longer. . . . And money was food" (40). Like Abe Jenkins in *Parched Earth*, and like the migrants of *The Grapes of Wrath*, the man from Kansas was once a small farmer. While Huxley's narrator partly blames the man's own mismanagement of his affairs for his misfortunes, he adds that "California" (elsewhere the narrator specifically mentions the California tycoon Jo Stoyte who employs the migrants) bears the responsibility for reducing the migrants to a condition of "wandering peonage" (94-95). Until the novel's prophet-figure, William Propter, comes to his rescue, the man from Kansas lived in a hovel on Stoyte's estate, unable properly to support his three malnourished children. When the Jetts of Sinclair's *Co-op* arrive in the California town of San Sebastian, they learn that it is not "the Sunshine City of the Golden State" with "golden pavements" they had imagined (101, 97). They find it to be "exactly like other cities of America," a "cold and hostile place, in which they took their chances with a million others in the same plight" (102, 103). The "Golden State" of California is "just one of forty-eight which had been caught in a depression . . . overfull of hungry and frightened people, wandering here and there, looking for something different, and finding the same thing" (99). Although the Jetts receive generous treatment from individuals, the official policy of town governments toward the homeless unemployed is one of a grudging charity, designed to shift responsibility for their needs onto neighboring communities. The migrants receive just enough gasoline to carry them to the next town, and "enough food to make it certain that if they died it would be of something else than starvation" (101). When Cristy Jett goes into an elegant restaurant in San Sebastian to ask for food, the proprietor tries to have him arrested for begging (105). As in other fiction of the period, California parodies the Promised Land of the migrants' dreams.

In the fictional world of the four Depression-era California novels, natural abundance and monopoly of the land's resources equal hunger for the propertyless. In the words of the narrator in *The Grapes of Wrath*, where a man is not allowed to "pick an orange for a thin child," yet oranges may be dumped as garbage with a drop in their market price, "a fallow field is a sin" (257-58). The monopolization of the land's resources in all three novels is shown as leading not to the satisfaction of basic human needs through more efficient production, but to waste and widespread hunger. Probably the best known passage in all California literature on the process whereby hunger grows in the land of plenty is that in the narrative interchapter of *The Grapes of Wrath* (just before the chapter in which the Joads leave the Weedpatch federal camp for the exploitative fruit ranch at Pixley). The passage opens with a lovingly detailed description of seasonal growth in the fruit orchards—of the flowering season, followed by the time when "Grape blossoms shed their tiny petals and the hard little beads become green buttons, and the buttons grow heavy. . . . The year is heavy with produce" (383). Abundance and fertility quickly turn to decay, as the fruit for which the grower can obtain little or no commercial profit is allowed to rot. The tragedy of waste is recounted in a prose rhythm reminiscent of Old Testament prophetic literature, which recalls the original "land of milk and honey" of which the California of *The Grapes of Wrath* is a parody: "The decay spreads over the State, and the sweet smell is a great sorrow on the land" (384).[5]

As the narrator contrasts the "fertile" earth and the "sturdy" trees of California's orchards with the deformity of a system which obliges children to die of pellagra "because a profit cannot be taken from an orange," the interchapter closes with a jeremiad-like warning: "In the eyes of the people there is the failure; and in the eyes of the hungry there is a growing wrath. In the souls of the people the grapes of wrath are filling and growing heavy, growing heavy for the vintage" (385).

This warning immediately follows the scene at the Weedpatch camp where, as the story of the rubber workers' collective show of strength in the Akron turkey shoot is told, the listening migrants begin to realize their own potential to defend themselves against intimidation by California landowners: "All our folks got guns . . . maybe we ought to get up a turkey shootin' club . . ." (381). In the chapter which follows the narrator's "jeremiad" Tom Joad meets up again with Jim Casy, now leading a strike and preaching collective action. Tom Joad takes up the idea: "I been thinkin' how it was in the gov'ment camp, how our folks took care a theirselves . . . . I been a-wonderin' why we can't do that all over. Throw out the cops that ain't our people. All work together for our own thing . . . farm our own lan'" (463).

Similar developments take place in *Parched Earth*, where the novel's labor leader and prophet-figure Dave Washburn begins to organize the Tontos Valley cannery workers, and preaches working-class solidarity to the hoboes and migrant workers riding the freights into the town of Caldwell. Even in *After Many a Summer* the desperate economic situation of the migrants provides the context for their organization into a community by the novel's prophet-figure, William Propter.

Poverty in the midst of plenty provides the impetus for organization of a community by the residents of "Pipe City" in *Co-op*. The cooperative of Sinclair's novel differs somewhat from those of *Parched Earth*, *The Grapes of Wrath* and *After Many a Summer*, in that its members include both homeless migrants, like the Jetts and the squatters of Pipe City, and unemployed residents of the town of San Sebastian. Its members will eventually include a former marketing executive, a doctor, an unemployed university professor, gardeners, nurses, clerical workers and musicians. Like the more homogeneous groups of *Parched Earth* and *The Grapes of Wrath*, this heterogeneous group is brought together by common need, in a wealthy community which regards their plight with indifference, and in the context of an economic system characterized by waste and inefficiency (303).

Crucial as economic circumstances in these novels are, however, they are not the only factor in the growth of social cooperation and/or collective action in the four novels. The most casual reading makes clear how central the California agrarian setting itself is to this development. The setting not only provides the pretext, in the context of each narrative, for a group of isolated, uprooted strangers to find themselves together under conditions of extreme physical hardship, but also provides a setting in which the prophet-figure can secure a hearing. When Dave Washburn, the prophet-figure of *Parched Earth*, first preaches to Hop Collins on the roof of the Caldwell-bound train, the hoboes laugh at him (138). His organizing efforts in the town of Caldwell itself are largely a failure. The turning-point only occurs after the workers are evicted from their cabins on Everett Caldwell's premises. As homeless campers with nothing further to lose, they finally give ear to Washburn's speech about class solidarity and "building for a new day," and find the courage to defend Washburn against an assault by Wally, their employer's physically threatening idiot son, and the wisdom to understand that this figure representative of capitalism can only be overpowered through collective action (191-96). Similarly, Jim Casy only fulfills his prophet's vocation in the rural setting of a migrant fruit-pickers' camp. At the start of the Joads' journey to California he is not even welcomed by all the members of the family. To Al, as driver and mechanic, Casy is merely potentially harmful deadweight in the car: "We'll burn right up if we got climbin' to do. Have to throw out some a' this stuff. Maybe we shouldn' a brang that preacher" (134). On the way to California Casy performs specific acts of service to individuals—praying, at Granma's insistence, for the dying Grampa, offering himself for arrest in the place of Tom Joad; but it is in the context of the strike at the Hooper ranch that Casy is chosen to lead a group—where he is finally able, in fact, to articulate the utopia of mutual support that he had been striving to formulate from the novel's first pages (422).

In *After Many a Summer* the migrant camp setting has a slightly different function from that which it performs in *Parched Earth* and *The Grapes of Wrath*. It is, as in the other two novels, a context for the growth of a community among the migrant workers. It also invites contrast with the claustrophobic setting of Jo Stoyte's castle-museum. The latter, with its massive size and impenetrable security, serves as an image of Stoyte's domineering and suspicious ego—of imprisonment in that ego (147). All the castle's inhabitants—the literary scholar Pordage, the cynical Dr. Obispo, and Stoyte's naively narcissistic mistress Virginia Maunciple—are likewise portrayed as suffering in varying degrees from what Robert Baker has called "a kind of spiritual agoraphobia" (195). Propter, by contrast, dwells not in the castle's cluttered interior, but in a bungalow near the castle. In fact, Propter seems to spend most of his time out of doors. The interior of his house is never even described. His typical habitat is a bench in a eucalyptus grove where he sits to instruct the Okies, Pete Boone, the young communist who eventually becomes one of his disciples, and the skeptical scholar Pordage on the way to attain religious transcendence, as well as in the construction of communes.[6]

In *Co-op*, the rural surroundings of San Sebastian are presented as a crucial factor in the cooperative's economic success. The cultivated land on the town's edges offers the cooperators access to surplus produce, which they use as the initial basis of barter in their "Self-Help Exchange" (137). The cooperative's members offer farm labor on local ranches in exchange for crops which "face a glutted market" and would otherwise be destroyed (144). They plant vegetables on plots loaned to them by wealthy landowners (128).

It is only through access to the rural/agricultural settings, in fact, that the prophet-figures succeed in communicating their utopian messages at all. The town-dwellers of *Parched Earth*, small businesspeople who are largely presented as small-minded and greedy, regard the proletariat as a potentially dangerous rabble and men like Dave Washburn as rabble-rousers. Apart from the fact that they are destroyed by an engulfing flood, the novel's metaphor for the revolution to come, they are hardly probable converts, in any case, to Washburn's marxist utopia. Steinbeck's city people are depicted as cut off from contact with working-class people, but also from "sun and wind and earth" (169). The characters in Stoyte's castle in *After Many a Summer* are variously cut off from the castle's rural/agricultural surroundings. Stoyte is alienated by his obsession with acquiring property and his hatred for the migrants who work for him; his doctor, Obispo, by his obsession with knowledge as power; Jeremy Pordage by his preoccupation with words and with literary scholarship; Stoyte's mistress, Virginia, by her lack of interest in anything beyond her immediate self-gratification. Only Pete Boone conceives of a more harmonious and cooperative form of social organization than that to be found in the Stoyte castle. To realize his vision he has to step outside the castle walls and spend his days with Propter at the commune among the eucalyptus trees. The citizens of San Sebastian in *Co-op* are presented as, in general, favorably disposed toward the founding of the new cooperative, but their goodwill would be of little value without the plots of land for farming and gardening which the well-wishers make available. Unlike the artificial setting of Southern California, which is also depicted in *After Many a Summer*, and unlike that of the Hollywood of *The Day of the Locust* (discussed in Chapter Four), the California rural/agricultural setting is, it seems, to some extent idealized as possessing, in its "organic" naturalness, a power to heal and transform human society that the "artificial" urban world lacks. If California represents a parody of Canaan, it is a parody which is capable of being transformed through a group's adoption of utopian ideals, in a way that California's "Natural Museum" is not.

In this adoption of and practice of utopian ideals, the prophet-figure and the group in the three novels inspire, activate and motivate one another. In the words of Mannheim:

> Only when the utopian conception of the individual seizes upon currents already present in society and gives expression to them, when in this form it flows back into the outlook of the whole group, and is translated into action by it, only then can the existing order be challenged by the striving for another order of existence. (207)

As in the historical setting of the California migrant labor situation, in the fiction of the period the emergence of prophet-figures follows a collective crisis of faith in the California Dream. Self-appointed and/or popularly chosen prophet-figures arise only after circumstances have created a role and function for them. The prophet-figure is, in the words of Steinbeck's narrator, as much a result of social circumstances as a cause: "Paine, Marx, Jefferson, Lenin, were results, not causes . . ." (166). William Propter is moved by the exploitation of migrants on Jo Stoyte's estate. Dave Washburn, the Communist activist in *Parched Earth*, becomes a credible leader of the cannery workers only after their eviction from company housing and a lockout at the cannery. Jim Casy gradually finds his vocation after the Oklahoma tenant farmers have become homeless migrants on the road. Charlie Day and Sigvald Soren, unemployed, act in response to their own economic plight and that of others, seeking, like other members of the cooperative "some way to exist without . . . cheating and destroying their fellow men and women" (216).

Clearly, a prophet needs followers—individuals in whom, as Mannheim suggests, existing social "currents" already flow, and who are therefore receptive to whatever utopian conception the prophet is able to offer them. Ideas of social cooperation spread "horizontally" among the members of social groups, sometimes independently of the prophet-figure's specific preaching. In *Parched Earth*, for instance, the train guard Hop Collins is already shown experiencing a change in his social attitudes, even before he comes directly under Dave Washburn's influence. As economic depression becomes a factor affecting ever more lives, he modifies his behavior toward the hoboes illegally riding on "his" train: "Once Hop would have called them bums, but these were depression times and pretty nearly everybody was a bum or on his way to becoming one. . . . A few years ago he would have snarled abuse at them and reached for his club" (137). Now Hop disobeys the company rules and tolerates the hoboes. Similarly, Tom Joad, long before he becomes a convert to Casy's faith in "one big soul," and a labor activist striving to practice Casy's teachings, conceives, independently of Casy, of the notion of collective labor action: ". . . 'spose them people got together an' says, 'Let the peaches rot.' Wouldn' be long 'fore the price went up . . ." (271). The other members of the Joad family also learn various lessons of cooperation as they move on the road. After Grampa Joad dies in the Wilsons' tent, the two families share what Pa Joad calls "almost a kin bond" (183). Other families share gasoline with the Joads, as two families drive out together to look for work on California farms (283, 465). In *Co-op*, the shared experiences of individuals economically and socially dependent upon one another make of the cooperative a community, where the hardships and anxieties inflicted by the Depression can be publicly discussed: "Here was a place where everybody was poor. Those who worked here talked about it openly, and made a joke of things which before could hardly be spoken out loud." The cooperative members find in the "co-op" not only a source of subsistence for their families, but also "courage, and good-fellowship" (176). The cooperative members help to deliver the Jetts' baby, when Mel Jett goes into labor on their doorstep, and the Jetts in gratitude donate the townspeople's gifts to the cooperative (115). The men of the cooperative all join the comic demonstration of growing their hair to protest the restrictive state laws which have put their barber out of business, and succeed in persuading the authorities to allow him to reopen (150-52). They share the grief at the tragic suicide of one of their members (379). These developments are "spontaneous," in the sense that they arise from the dictates of circumstance rather than from a basis in any specific utopian theoretical conception.

On the other hand, the prophet-figures, in giving explicit theoretical formulation to a specific utopian ideal, supply the group with motivation to continue and develop their impulses toward mutually supportive behavior as a matter of conscious and deliberate choice. This is clear in the respect with which the evicted cannery workers listen to Dave Washburn's homily on proletarian solidarity: "Chinese or Italian, Negro or German—they're all the same if they're workingmen" (191). It is evident in Tom's reflections on Casy's words after Casy's death (which Tom had resisted paying attention to while the prophet was alive): "I know now a fellow ain't no good alone" (462). It is apparent, too, in the description of the process by which William Propter begins to teach the man from Kansas to "think a bit more realistically . . . about the world of everyday life," (with a view, eventually, to educating him about the possibility of religious transcendence) (98). In *Co-op*, the cooperative members listen attentively to organizer Charlie Day, who calls upon them to "build something more powerful than any of them could alone" (48). They are inspired by the "old-time gospel fervor" of the Reverend Elias Prosser, who regards the rescue of the destitute through EPIC as "a new method of saving souls" (223), and by Sigvald Soren's exhortations to loyalty to the cooperative, and to mutual aid (300).

The teachings of the prophet-figures result directly in a number of concrete actions. Among these may be counted Hop Collins' preaching of Dave Washburn's message of proletarian solidarity to Hattie Rathbone and her mother. Collins not only expresses admiration for Washburn, but invokes an idealized version of North America's pioneering past very different from that of the frontier individualism depicted by R.W.B. Lewis or Henry Nash Smith. Hop explicitly rejects the notion that the early pioneers were totally self-sufficient individualists: "They were people that cooperated with each other. . . . They kept thinkin' about their neighbors as well as themselves" (150). Hop claims to observe, in the harsh conditions of the Depression, the development of a renewed spirit of cooperation, in the form of worker solidarity: "Us workin' men is getting back some of that pioneer spirit of standin' together that was lost when folks like Everett Caldwell got the upper hand" (150). Later in the novel a group of workers, Washburn's disciples, help one another climb to safety from the flood that engulfs the Tontos Valley. The result of this act of mutual assistance is that they will be able to share the "rich harvest" that awaits them after the flood subsides.

In *The Grapes of Wrath* Tom decides to become a labor organizer, like Casy before him. Rose of Sharon feeds the starving migrant. In *After Many a Summer* the man from Kansas is first introduced as a bitter, misanthropic individual, who compensates himself for his suffering, in the words of the narrator, "by brutality to those weaker than himself," bullying his wife and beating his children, whom he resents as an economic burden (40). Four chapters later, he occupies a cabin in Propter's little commune, and shares the produce of its garden (93). The San Sebastian Self-Help Exchange of Upton Sinclair's *Co-op* is traced in its growth from a membership of dozens to one of hundreds. Moreover, just as a number of inhabitants of Pipe City follow Charlie Day into founding the San Sebastian Self-Help Exchange, so two of the cooperative's members later decide to campaign for the EPIC program, after hearing the Reverend Elias Prosser preach his "crusade" to end poverty in the state of California (218).

The growth of various forms of supportive or cooperative behavior in all three novels is not without setbacks. In *Parched Earth* the cannery workers are routed by a gang of thugs outside the Caldwell factory, and even Dave Washburn is unable to rally them until later, in their makeshift camp under the trees. In *The Grapes of Wrath* a number of such setbacks occur; as when Ma Joad, moved by an irresistible sense of obligation, feeds another woman's children, only to find she has painfully wounded their mother's pride (285). Again, when the Joads' neighbors fail to escape from the encroaching flood at Pixley because they stayed to help build a protective dam while Rose of Sharon gave birth, they turn on Pa Joad and blame him (490). Yet the overall development of the novel suggests that these lapses in cooperation are temporary. As Ma Joad says, shortly before the closing scene in which she urges Rose of Sharon to give her breast to the starving stranger, "Use' ta be the family was fust. It ain't so now. It's anybody" (491). The migrant in *After Many a Summer* is skeptical and suspicious of Propter and of his paradoxical sayings, even shocked by his apparent lack of reverence for Scripture (94). Yet he moves into Propter's little commune, and even begins to listen to Propter's teaching. In the long run, Propter believes, the man from Kansas may come to adopt not only Propter's way of life on the land, but also his religious philosophy. In *Co-op*, too, setbacks arise as a result of human failings. The cooperative's members have to contend with their own inexperience in the performance of the "hundreds of little jobs" necessary if the cooperative is to function (190-91). They encounter the incomprehension of new members, who at first fail to understand that the "co-ordinators" are not their "bosses" but their servants and their elected representatives (173). Friction arises between Charlie Day and Sigvald

Soren, over Sig's unsought popularity with malcontents who beg him to take over Day's position (224). However, Sig avoids a potentially damaging conflict by transferring to work outside the cooperative for the EPIC campaign, which will benefit the cooperative movement as a whole (230). The public airing of grievances leads to increased, not diminished, cohesion. The community emerges strengthened from such tests (193).

A further crucial question for all four fictional utopias is whether a utopia based on cooperation, mutuality or solidarity can be perpetuated after the conditions of deprivation which first created the need for it have been alleviated. For all four narrators this question is closely tied to that of control of a given society's wealth; but also specifically to its means of production, and above all, to its machines.

Concern about the role to be occupied by technology in the rural/agricultural setting is hardly a new one for American literature, as Leo Marx has long since demonstrated.[7] The four novels currently under study, like earlier works, deal with the question of "the machine in the garden"—but with the important difference from many earlier works that the pastoral serenity which the machine disrupts in nineteenth-century fiction has already been undercut in *The Grapes of Wrath*, *Parched Earth*, *After Many a Summer* and *Co-op* by the prior existence of deprivation and hunger. The machine, in the form of a train, an automated canning plant or a tractor, in California's garden in these novels enters a world in which pastoral serenity has already been shattered by the disillusionment of the pastoral's inhabitants. The machine is not presented as a threat *per se* but as a metaphor for the dehumanizing and destructive nature of predatory individualism; and above all, as a power which should be controlled by the many rather than the few. The question of human ownership and control of technology, and of how that control and ownership are exercised, is presented therefore as of paramount significance. The machine may have entered the garden—entered it, like the tractor in *The Grapes of Wrath*, in the form of a monster—but it remains potentially capable of subjection to the service of collective human needs.

In *Parched Earth* the machine as monster—and also what Steinbeck's narrator calls the danger of "machines in private hands"—

are illustrated by Everett Caldwell's use of automation in his canning plant to rid himself of dependence on the mutinous seasonal cannery workers. This move by Caldwell to introduce machinery is explicitly presented by the novel's narrator as a further extension of the "upper hand" as Hop Collins calls it, of control not only over the cannery workers, but over the local community as a whole (150). Caldwell uses the automation of his plant to free himself of the need for manual workers, but also to exact revenge on Belle Vasquez, mother of his illegitimate child and hence a source of embarrassment to him. Belle's loss of the custom of the workers on whom she depends for her living as a prostitute serves from one perspective as a further example of the extension and intensification of the capitalist's power through the use of technology. The object of condemnation does not appear to be the use of technology in itself—the survivors of the flood which engulfs the town of Caldwell at the novel's close are the inheritors of all the area's resources (assuming they are still usable after having been submerged by the flood)—but its monopolization, to the disadvantage of the majority. Even in the seemingly most deterministic use of technological metaphor in the novel, when the crashing of a train in the Caldwell railroad yard is used to suggest the inevitable fate of American capitalism, the accident is shown to have occurred through the negligence of Everett Caldwell's managers.[8] Again, individual responsibility and control are presented as of paramount importance. If capitalism is to destroy itself, the main cause of its destruction, in Armstrong's version of the marxian "providential fable" will be not only technological and economic, but also human.

In *The Grapes of Wrath*, too, the machine may be regarded as destructive or benign, depending upon who controls it. In the celebrated description of the tractor tearing up the Oklahoma land the machine is, it is true, characterized as a monster which has by extension dehumanized its operator, "goggled" his mind and "muzzled his protest" against the inhumanity of the tenant farmers' eviction. Yet the conclusion reached by the watching farmer awaiting his dispossession is that the real monster is the large capitalist. A human being owning property on an impersonal scale—"property he doesn't see, or can't take time to get his fingers in, or can't be there to walk on"—becomes dehumanized and "the servant of his property" (37-39).[9] The tractor merely represents the prior dehumanization which is represented as being the fate of "the great owners." Unlike, say, the machine in an earlier California novel, Frank Norris' *The Octopus*, the tractor could be turned from its path.[10] "It's not like lightning or earthquake," the representative farmer in *The Grapes of Wrath* reflects, "We've got a bad thing made by men, and by God that's something we can change" (41). Later in the novel, one page after Ma Joad has been shown predicting, "A different time's comin'," the narrator expresses the view that the migrants' helplessness in their altered social situation stems partly from the fact that they have had little or no prior experience of "the power and danger of machines in private hands" (311). The novel leaves the reader without any concrete proposal for the integration of the machine into its utopia of cooperation. However, the narrator's ideal is apparently for the migrants to become smallholders, if on a more cooperative basis. Great owners are warned that "when property accumulates in too few hands it is taken away" (263). Yet the possibility of integration of technology into the new society which the narrator envisages as coming into being out of the mass displacement of the tenant farmer is hinted at:

> Is a tractor bad? Is the power that turns the long furrows wrong? If this tractor were ours it would be good—not mine, but ours. If our tractor turned the long furrows of our land, it would be good. Not my land, but ours. We could love this tractor then as we have loved this land when it was ours. . . . (165).

The narrator indicates, if only in general terms, the direction toward which social organization and the control of technology are to move—away from individual or corporate monopoly, towards greater sharing of property, including technology.

The utopia of *After Many a Summer* also emphasizes decentralized control of technology as a precondition for a more cooperative, humane society. If William Propter experiments with intermediate technology—a point which will be addressed in due course—he shows himself equally concerned with questions of human social organization. The ideal social system, Propter suggests, would be one in which a Jo Stoyte would be discouraged from being "greedy and domineering"—traits on which, in

Propter's view, the existing socioeconomic system "puts a premium" (147-48). The real problem, as he himself readily admits, lies not in the uncontrollability of technology, but in the reluctance of human beings so to control it. To cover California with cooperatives sharing the collective wealth and heavily dependent upon intermediate technology would of course require "the permission of the banks" (243). Propter shares with the narrators of *Parched Earth* and *The Grapes of Wrath*, however, the basic conception that control over technology must be decentralized as a precondition for a cooperative utopia that will also be fully democratic.

For the members of the Self-Help Exchange in *Co-op*, as for the seekers of a utopia in the other novels with rural/agricultural settings, shared ownership of the machine transforms it from a generator of unemployment, to a means of developing a self-sustaining democratic community. For example, members of the cooperative take pleasure and pride in using the electrical saw which they have acquired by bartering their labor. To a member of the cooperative who observes their work, the fact that the workers "own the tool they are working with" means that "the produce will be ours" and used for the benefit of all the cooperative's participants, instead of for the profit of one individual (131). The people involved in the cooperative, by "working for themselves" are able to make the machine work for them (410).

Each of the aspects of technology dealt with in the novels of Armstrong, Steinbeck, Huxley, and Sinclair, functions in fictional terms as an image of the inhumane, destructive power of predatory capitalism. Insofar as each presents a utopia the suggestion, implicit or explicit, is that there may indeed be ways to "civilize the machine."[11]

The four novelists all present characters whose disillusionment, their experience of hunger amid plenty, brings them to the conception of a transformation of existing society, partly through a change in society's use of technology. Within this common ground, the prophet-figures' respective utopias exhibit a number of important differences. These differences concern not only the views and actions adopted by characters in the novels, but also the ways in which the California rural/agricultural setting is presented, the differences in attitudes to the uses of technology expressed, the degree of conflict with the power of capital which takes place in each novel, and even perhaps the degree of success which is envisaged as possible for each of the prophet-figures' utopias.

Major differences are apparent in the roles played by each of the prophet-figures—differences which in turn have implications for each novel's treatment of setting. Dave Washburn's marxism, Jim Casy's utopia of community and mutuality, William Propter's transcendental anarchism, the "reciprocal economy" of Charlie Day and Sigvald Soren, have particular effects on the ways in which both landscape and narrative in the agrarian setting are presented.

The alienation of the dispossessed from the California Dream, which formerly had seemed likely to offer them a share, however meager, in the land's abundance, sets up a dialectic between collective aspiration and collective disillusionment. One possible synthesis, as presented in the work of Armstrong, Steinbeck, Huxley, and Sinclair, is to be found in the quest for utopia that may wholly or in part substitute for the ideology of the Dream to which the dispossessed had formerly subscribed. However, the narrators in *Parched Earth*, *The Grapes of Wrath*, *After Many a Summer*, and *Co-op* manipulate the degree to which the dispossessed are portrayed as seeking radically utopian solutions to their predicament. *Parched Earth* has a Communist prophet-figure—although his followers among the workers are shown achieving little of a radical nature at all; and indeed the practical question of *how* society is to be transformed is, as Edwin Seaver pointed out in 1934, largely sidestepped by employing as a metaphor of social revolution a catastrophic flood which drowns the Tontos Valley and the capitalists living in it.[12] In *The Grapes of Wrath*—despite Stoddard Martin's contention that the novel's narrator advocates socialism,[13] and despite some indication in Steinbeck's work of a dialogue with the American Left—the most radical idea explicitly entertained by the prophet-figure Jim Casy or by Tom Joad his disciple is one of collective action to defeat the power of the big landowners and to enable the Okies to become smallholders. In *After Many a Summer* William Propter's ideal—of a community of migrants living in self-sufficient independence of industrial capitalism—is in some ways more radically utopian than Steinbeck's "Jeffersonian" agrarianism; but it is also a solution which is not the organically developed conception of the migrants themselves, but rather of a philanthropic benefactor external to their group. Above all, Propter's utopia is presented as a solution to the needs of a few individuals or families only, not to those of a society or even of California's migrants in general. (A marxist utopia, for example, is expressly critiqued and rejected.) Huxley's "philosophic anarchism,"[14] as he refers to it in a 1938 letter to his brother Julian, is in the last analysis as much influenced by the popularizer of mysticism and yogic techniques, Gerald Heard, as it is by the social theories of Borsodi. Its central aim is to bring about the social conditions which would best favor "self-transcendence," rather than the creation of a utopian social organization as an end in itself. In a number of respects, the utopia of *Co-op* is presented as having greater potential to alter the socioeconomic system broadly and permanently, than the utopias of *Parched Earth*, *The Grapes of Wrath* and *After Many a Summer.* Like Propter's community, it involves a group of people who successfully make part of their living from it, but it is involved with a broader social and material economy (that of the town of San Sebastian) in a way that Propter's community is not. Moreover, the San Sebastian Self-Help Exchange represents one of fifty consumer cooperatives and "nearly a hundred credit unions" in California which serve as examples to the rest of the nation (378). It is presented as having the backing of a minority of bureaucrats in the New Deal administration who lobby for it (if not altogether successfully), and the support of the EPIC movement. At least in the narrator's view, it represents the trend of the future. According to Sigvald Soren, "The men who are now guiding a few thousand workers will have to be guiding as many hundred thousand in a short time—perhaps by the end of this decade" (317). In his opinion, "Co-operation is the coming idea" (318). Unlike Propter's utopia, in that of Sigvald Soren and Charlie Day, the creation of cooperatives is very much an end in itself, providing a model for the new cooperative socialist society.

These differences in utopian conception are not without implications for the differing ways in which landscape is depicted in the four novels. While they share the image of California's garden as a parody of Eden or of Canaan, the manner of depiction appears to vary at least partly according to the form of utopia presented.

In *Parched Earth* the rural landscape is sketched in with very little detail. Buildings—Caldwell's New England-style mansion, which represents his role in the novel as "Yankee capitalist"; Belle

Vasquez's hovel, which suggests the decline of Spanish feudal power; Hattie Rathbone's home by the railroad tracks, which provides a safe refuge for the proletariat in time of danger—serve as metaphors of the class struggle. Appropriately, perhaps, for a novel which celebrates the triumph of the proletariat, images of "nature" in *Parched Earth* are largely related to work of some kind—the "golden fruit which hangs on branches awaiting pails and hands"; the descriptions of the processes of pitting apricots and preserving them with sulphur; of the rains falling on the dry Tontos Valley, whose main significance is the "abundant harvests" they will make possible. Description of landscape, what little there is of it, is always strictly functional, made to serve the needs of Armstrong's marxist fable (141, 309).

Descriptions of nature in *The Grapes of Wrath*, with a few exceptions, tend to focus on the near point—sunlight on grape leaves (327), or prunes lengthening "like little green bird's eggs" (383), or "the black lumps of haycocks" seen by starlight (41). This concern with detail seems directly related to the novel's emphasis on an organic, intimate, loving relationship with the land, which ideally is a source not only of economic but of emotional nourishment. This emphasis on emotional ties to the land further distinguishes *The Grapes of Wrath* from both *Parched Earth* and *After Many a Summer*. For Armstrong's workers an extension of access to possession of the land is important for the improved material conditions such access will create for them. For Huxley's migrants—at least as William Propter views the matter—access to shared use of the land is merely a precondition for the material and psychological independence necessary to religious self-transcendence. For Steinbeck's displaced tenant farmers a return to access to an adequate standard of living is important, obviously; but the narrator makes clear that the possibility of return to the lost connection with the land is important, too. The narrator goes so far as to claim, implausibly, that the land may actually die under ploughing by a hired hand on a machine who feels no such emotional connection: "The land bore under iron, and under iron gradually died; for it was not loved or hated, it had no prayers or curses" (88). Thus the descriptions of spring in California—of "first tendrils of the grapes swelling from the old gnarled vines," of "spindly" cauliflower plants and "short, lean wheat," or of bay horses "In the stiff pull straining hams and buttocks, split-second timed together," sold to finance the trip to California, are crucial in building the case for restoring the broken tie to the land. This tie is presented as being economic, but also moral and emotional (382-83, 94).

In direct contrast to Steinbeck's descriptions in *The Grapes of Wrath*, those in *After Many a Summer* are remarkable for the extent to which they depend upon presentation from a distance. What is most interesting about them, though, are the ways in which they serve as an index of the characters' understanding, or lack of understanding, of Propter's utopia. For Jeremy Pordage, for instance, the skeptical British scholar, the California landscape is a geometric enigma. Pordage sees the plain around Los Angeles from the hills above, "chequered" with green patches (14). During his drive to Stoyte's castle he notes orchards "mathematically planted" in rows that allow him a bewildering succession of glimpsed perspectives as the car passes (15), and then a line of mountains rising above the orange groves, tracing an "uninterpretable graph of boom and slump" (15). For Pordage the mathematical symmetry of the landscape represents an enigma he finds himself powerless to interpret. He takes refuge from the strangeness of his surroundings in literary allusion, reassured when he can "pigeonhole" the spreading miles of orange groves in terms of a quotation from Marvell's "Bermudas." Yet given the actual plight of the migrants, who will shortly be introduced in the novel, the lines about God's benign provision of oranges to shipwrecked believers are an evasion of the enigma. The problem is as follows: if orange groves are planted in regimented lines and fields laid out like a chess board, the being ultimately responsible for bringing this symmetry about is not God, but the novel's tycoon, Jo Stoyte, who is shown reaching out his long arm of economic possession to buy up further land for development (32-33).

For Stoyte the land is, like his oil and his gravesites in the Beverly Pantheon, merely another commodity for his enrichment. For his mistress, Virginia, who never seems to step outside the castle grounds, it is a playground for her personal enjoyment. For the man from Kansas, the novel's representative Dust Bowl migrant, depicted as wholly preoccupied with the immediate question of his own and his family's survival, the landscape as object of contemplation hardly exists. His children's wonder at their new surroundings is merely an excuse for him to vent his exasperation by hitting them (41). Each of these characters is presented as sharing with Jeremy Pordage an inability to understand the significance of the landscape, a knowledge to which William Propter alone holds the key.

For Propter, the world of time and appearance is an "idiot universe," which the enlightened individual who has transcended attachment to the ego will spontaneously perceive as such. Hence for Propter the orchards and mountains surrounding the Stoyte castle are not to be dwelt upon in intellectual puzzlement, nor treated as commodities, nor valued for the sensuous pleasure they provide; but rather to be viewed both as part of the furnishing of an absurd world of time and as a means to an end. The chiaroscuro of the mountains at sunset, visible from the bench outside Propter's house, serves the prophet-figure as an image of the religious transcendence he seeks, and hence as an aid to meditation. Through focusing his attention on the rural landscape and achieving a mood of serenity before concentrating his mind within, Propter is able to attain an altered state of consciousness in which he is freed from the burden of the ego.[15]

It is this transcendent awareness that Propter's small commune is designed to help others achieve. His concern with the land is therefore as practical in its way as Dave Washburn's; yet his attitude to "nature" is very different from either Washburn's or Jim Casy's. Propter is as concerned with the landscape as a means to the development of altered consciousness as he is with the material sustenance to be drawn from the land. Material concerns are not disregarded in *After Many a Summer*, however. The image of the mountains which, as seen through Jeremy Pordage's eyes, trace a graph of economic indicators against the sky, thus invites the reader to acknowledge economic terms in Huxley's utopia, even if economic needs are to be subordinated to "spiritual" ones.

The descriptions of landscape in *Co-op* are as few and as brief as in *Parched Earth*, but serve a somewhat different function. Apart from explaining the workings of cooperative market gardening they present images of a pastoral ideal depicted as integral to the cooperative project. This "Indigent Idyll," as it is called in the title of Chapter Five of *Co-op*, is evoked in a few sentences about

"California's foothills carpeted golden with poppies and little suncups; pink and blue with gillias and wild lilacs," or about an orchard after rain, "covered with a thick carpet of the brightest green" (234, 129). The emotional ties of the cooperative members with the land and the produce they grow on it are only once described more specifically, in terms which invite comparison with Steinbeck: "When . . . you have sweated in the sun and tended young plants . . . and wangled old building lath from the school board and wire from the telephone company, and tied up the vines . . . and watched the crop through storm and drought . . . tomatoes begin to acquire a meaning to you." The narrator continues, "You see the fruit hanging from the vines by thousands; they grow bigger and smoother and shinier every day; until the time when they begin to turn from green to red." Even in this idyllic pastoral description, the narrator does not omit reference to the daily struggles of the cooperative for scarce resources. After supplies for growing the tomatoes have been "wangled" from local institutions and the fruit successfully cultivated, there remain the questions of "whether the contact section has found markets, and whether there are going to be enough lugs and jars, and trucks, and labour." The narrator points a moral for middle-class readers, who may learn, like the middle-class participants in the cooperative, "how working-people pay for what they get in this world" (265). The descriptions of rural settings in *Co-op* thus combine the emphasis on emotional ties to the land of *The Grapes of Wrath* with the functional account of agricultural labor in *Parched Earth*. In the account of the struggle for survival of the cooperative utopia, its "indigence" and the practical necessities which govern its daily workings, are as much emphasized as its creation of a rural "idyll."

If differences between the utopias of *Parched Earth*, *The Grapes of Wrath*, *After Many a Summer*, and *Co-op* affect the novels' treatments of the California landscape, they also lead to different perspectives on the best way to give the members of these potential utopias control over the machine. All four narrators regard the issue of control of technology as crucially important for the development of a viable utopia. They would probably not agree, however, over the precise form that control should take.

For Armstrong's narrator in *Parched Earth*, the monopoly of the novel's large capitalist Everett Caldwell over the Tontos Valley's resources, including technological resources, can be broken only by allowing the proletariat to possess them and benefit from them. There is no suggestion that the technology need be altered in any way; rather a change of ownership, a simple redistribution in the name of economic equality—and presumably, shared control of the means of production—will guarantee abundance, "a rich harvest," for all.

The Steinbeckian model of corporate capitalism, while it mystifies the corporation as "the monster," offers a somewhat more sophisticated view of the control of technology by banks and land companies than Armstrong's *Parched Earth*, with its melodramatic tycoon/villain. Steinbeck's "interchapters" differ crucially from *Parched Earth*, too, in their emphasis on the severance by foreclosures and evictions, of the tenant farmer's emotional tie to the land. In *Parched Earth* only Abe Jenkins expresses the sense of any such emotional tie. Like Steinbeck's Okies he is a small farmer. Not surprisingly, Armstrong's proletarians have no such bond to the land. In *The Grapes of Wrath* it is corporate absentee management that makes of the hired tractor driver a "machine man, driving a dead tractor on land he does not know and love" (126). Although in the early chapters of *The Grapes of Wrath* the "vitality" of working with a horse on a farm is clearly preferred to the "dead" quality of work with a tractor, the narrator finally achieves reconciliation with the machine by envisaging a shared, decentralized control of it. The tractor viewed as "our tractor" is apparently no longer the deadening destructive power it remains while in the control of the land company. Steinbeck's narrator stresses the "wonder" of personally working the land, which, it is claimed, leads to a "deep understanding" of it. At no point does the narrator inquire whether an urban small businessman might entertain similar feelings toward a store or a sweatshop. Steinbeck's organicist romanticism seems to have led to a certain confusion in his views about the role of technology in society. What is clearly not in dispute in *The Grapes of Wrath*, though, is the view, however simplistic, that control of the machine by small landholders is preferable to its control by a corporate oligarchy.

Huxley's *After Many a Summer* presents the most radical conception of possible change in the control, and also the form, of technology, within the context of a utopian vision. Paradoxically, although in practice Huxley's prophet-figure is highly skeptical about the possibility that his utopia will be adopted by society at large, his theoretical model for a reorganization of society goes beyond a change in control of the means of production to a more fundamental change, in the means of production themselves. William Propter's views on the use and control of technology closely follow those of Ralph Borsodi, whose School of Living at Suffern, New York, Huxley had visited a year before completing *After Many a Summer*. In a letter to Julian Huxley in April 1938, Aldous Huxley summarizes Borsodi's findings that "in 2/3 of the field of economics decentralized production in the home and the small workshop, using small power units and machines is from 20% to 35% cheaper than centralized mass production." As Grover Smith points out in his footnote to this letter, this is precisely the arrangement which William Propter advocates in *After Many a Summer* (434). Propter, however, seems to view with skepticism the likelihood of Californians adopting his proposal to "cover the state" with small townships and cooperatives employing intermediate technology (243). According to Propter the use of violence to effect social change is almost inevitably doomed to create for its users a set of social conditions at least as bad as those they set out to remedy.[16] Since he is at least sufficiently worldly-wise to know that the banks and corporations will not voluntarily assist a utopian program which threatens their own interests, he accepts the very limited scope for his experiment which this position inevitably entails: "All I expect is that, if I do my work and it's reasonably good, there'll be a few people who will want to collaborate with me" (149). The intermediate technology with which Propter works will remain a boon to the few.[17] It will, Propter foresees, function largely as an instrument in creating the social conditions he views as necessary for those few to attain "self-transcendence."

The cooperative members in *Co-op*, like the narrators in *Parched Earth* and *The Grapes of Wrath*, accept the benefits of existing technology, without any apparent wish to alter the form of the means of production. Collective control of technology is emphasized, in fact, even at the expense of productivity—a concession which neither Armstrong's narrator nor Steinbeck's, is willing to make. In the words of one of the cooperative members, as she explains members' reluctance to accept government grants for tools, if such assistance would mean loss of the cooperative's administrative autonomy, "We'd rather produce less, and have the tools in our own hands, and the control of them" (262). Although the long-term goal is for the unemployed to "get hold of . . . the tools" and "build themselves a new world," the narrator of *Co-op* is perhaps more realistic about the price of such independence in the short term.

At the same time, for the narrator of *Co-op* technology represents "the conquest of matter by mind," which eventually will enable the cooperative to produce a surplus "of all the material needs of its members." A cooperative member, evidently speaking on behalf of the narrator, suggests that social experiments are themselves analogous with innovations in technology. Both are "scientific." New forms of social organization resemble machines —"a lot of human beings put together in a certain way, to accomplish a certain purpose—just as the parts of the engine are put together to work in a certain way." With the speaker's final question, "If it is all right to invent machinery, why isn't it all right to invent new social forms?" the analogy between the literal machine and the metaphoric social machine becomes a justification of the utopian project itself (131-32).

Just as differences in the utopias of *Parched Earth*, *The Grapes of Wrath*, *After Many a Summer* and *Co-op* affect the conception of the human being's relation to the land and of the use and control of technology on the land, these differences affect the conception of the prophet-figure's role within the agrarian setting. That role includes his relation to his followers, the degree of conflict with the owners of the land which takes place in each novel, and even the degree of success which the narrator views as possible for the prophet's utopian ideal.

The relationship of the prophet-figure to his followers is partly determined by the degree to which each prophet-figure shares the class background and/or some of the ideological assumptions of the people he leads. These assumptions are to some extent dependent on the nature of the prophet-figure's utopia. Dave Washburn, for instance, is himself a migrant worker, who was an I.W.W. member before joining the Communist Party. In many ways his relationship of frankness and equality with the workers he leads recalls the version of the Communists' labor organizing practices described in the historical studies of 1930s California by Jackson J. Benson.[18] Jim Casy, on the other hand, who has the honored status of a former preacher of the Gospel and yet who lives in voluntary poverty (unlike other preachers he did not take up collections at prayer meetings), is both of the Okie community and yet set apart from it by his preacher's "calling." William Propter, the former university professor and inheritor of a modest private income, is the most "set apart" from those to whom he preaches, not only by his relative wealth but also by his transcendentalist approach to questions of social and political arrangements, an approach which, as the narrator makes clear, is far removed from the Bible Belt fundamentalism of the man from Kansas (97). The prophet-figures of *Co-op* are unusual, not only in that the preaching of utopia in the novel is performed by several figures rather than a single leader, but in the diversity of their backgrounds. Charlie Day is a former highly-paid publicity director to a company who has found himself destitute in Pipe City (7). The Reverend Elias Prosser is a liberal churchman who has "carried a message all his life" (218). Sigvald Soren is, in the narrator's words, an "Ex-sailor, ex-convict and builder of humanity," an unemployed resident of San Sebastian who makes a meager living out of seasonal labor, felling trees (7, 44). The range of occupations and social classes to be found among the prophet-figures of *Co-op* emphasizes the democratic, egalitarian and pluralistic nature of the cooperative experiment.

A digression seems appropriate here on a complicating factor in defining the relation between prophet-figure and followers in *The Grapes of Wrath* which does not operate in *Parched Earth*, *After Many a Summer* or *Co-op*: Steinbeck's notion of the phalanx. The phalanx is a "group-individual," which possesses autonomy and its own laws of motivation distinct from those of an individual human being. The leader is, to use Steinbeck's word, a specialized "function" of the group as a whole: "an expression of group-man, a cell endowed with a special function, like an eye cell, drawing . . . force from group-man, and at the same time directing him . . ." (145). In *In Dubious Battle*, published three years before *The Grapes of Wrath*, the actions of the phalanx are presented ambivalently. In the view of Doc Burton, one of the central characters and spokespersons of the novel, "Man hates himself,"[19] (253) and the group or "phalanx" is portrayed as prone to acts of irrational violence. In *The Grapes of Wrath*, where twenty families become one family as they travel on the road, the image of the phalanx is much more positive. The result of this bonding is not a lawless mob, but a community that almost instinctively establishes laws within and for itself (214). The shared features of the phalanx in *The Grapes of Wrath* and *In Dubious Battle*, however, are united action, arising spontaneously and as it were organically, in relation to which the leaders' apparently autonomous directives are a further spontaneously generated consequence.[20] Casy's rise to leadership in the strike at the Hooper ranch is a direct result of the group's pre-existent need for leaders. The coherence of the group during the protest he witnesses while in jail first gives him his cue to preaching his gospel of united action (422). It is true that Casy's "Emersonian" belief in "one big soul ever'body's a part of" (24) prepares him for the practical application of his faith in the "holiness" of the group as he travels with the migrants, fights for them and dies in their behalf. Yet in the last analysis, change will arise from the united action of the phalanx, more than from the directives of its leaders.[21] In *The Grapes of Wrath* it is the group which engenders and confirms the prophet-figure. The prophet-figure's role is to articulate and point the way toward a form of utopia which the group has already dimly intuited. Presumably, Armstrong's narrator believes this, too; but only Steinbeck's gives such a belief concrete expression.

Co-op also has its "collective mind," which the members observe "coming into being and learning to function," but it is utterly different from the phalanx of Steinbeck's fiction. The "collective mind" of *Co-op* has little to do with intuition, and a great deal to do with open public debate and democratic committee procedure: "Usually they didn't have to take a vote on propositions; they discussed them until everybody had had his say, and the sentiment had become unanimous" (137). If Charlie Day is "the driving force" of the cooperative enterprise, he is a democratic one. According to the narrator, the cooperative's organizers are "leaders without being dictators," managers of an institution in which government by consensus is the rule (319).

The mode by which cooperative groups confront the owners of the means of production and the degree of confrontation are closely related to the utopia preached in each of the four novels.

Yet the relationship is not always a simple one. In *Parched Earth*, for instance, the violent confrontation between labor and capital which one finds in many proletarian novels of the 1930s, does take place, as the evicted cannery workers, led by Dave Washburn, are routed by Caldwell's thugs at the cannery gates. However, although the author's marxist utopia expressly presupposes successful class conflict, the narrative presents incidents much less dramatic than had already occurred on the California scene, and the triumph of the proletariat is presented in purely figurative terms, through the device of a flood that foreshadows the anticipated proletarian revolution, but also forestalls the necessity for or possibility of any further class conflict in literal terms. *The Grapes of Wrath* portrays direct class conflict between organized groups only to a fairly limited extent in the narrative of the Joad family's experience, notably in the account of the strike at the Hooper ranch in which Casy is killed. The interchapters, though, are filled with a rhetoric of resistance and struggle: "Whyn't twenty of us take a piece of lan'? We got guns. Take it an' say, 'Put us off if you can.'" (260). The narrator endorses the migrants' fantasies through explicit comment: "And the association of owners knew that some day the praying would stop. And there's the end" (263). The cry of the evicted tenant farmer as paraphrased by the narrator is a version of the jeremiad: "You cut us down, and soon you will be cut down and there'll be none of us to save you" (94). A time will come, the narrator warns, when "the armies of bitterness will all be going the same way" (95). Steinbeck's narrator neither applauds nor wholly condemns the armed movement of the dispossessed which looms in the novel as a strong possibility. However, true to its New Deal ideology, *The Grapes of Wrath* indicates an alternative resolution of the migrants' situation in the form of federal government intervention—the migrant camp. Here the utopia of mutual support is relieved of its threatening aspect—its potential for issuing in overt class conflict—but also mixed with ideological elements, as the Okies are wooed and won over by the friendly, supportive camp manager, an employee of Roosevelt's New Deal administration. Class conflict on a wide scale remains largely an ever-present possibility rather than a fully realized eventuality.

In *After Many a Summer* confrontation between the migrant worker and the landowner does not arise. Propter intercedes for the migrants with Jo Stoyte's estate manager and with Stoyte himself, both of whom furiously resent Propter's interference and are apparently unconvinced by his appeal for an improvement in working conditions. The possibility of united action against Stoyte by the migrants themselves is not contemplated; and indeed Propter's reiterated insistence on the need for change in the individual as the source of change in society runs counter to any form of collective struggle. Only *Parched Earth* and *The Grapes of Wrath* envisage the possibility of direct conflict between the landowner and the agrarian dispossessed.

In *Co-op*, harmonious relations with local property owners are regarded as a precondition for the cooperative utopia's success. As Sig Soren points out to the organization's founders, the small group of businessmen who control the economy of San Sebastian have the power to "wipe out" the cooperative, "If we give them reason to fear us, or to hate us" (60). Rather than allow the local property owners to "harass" them "out of business," via their control of the law and the press, the cooperative's leaders make the pragmatic decision to trade with the capitalists through barter, and win their support (303). They persuade the businessmen that a cooperative of the unemployed is not a threat to private enterprise in the short run (although the long-term program of the cooperative movement is one of "starving" the capitalist system "out of existence") (157, 374). Sig Soren also plays skillfully upon the wealthy citizens' fears of popular unrest among the homeless and hungry: "If the unemployed could be allowed to trade for cabbages and beans and firewood, they would be too busy to listen to agitators and they wouldn't form mobs and riot in the streets" (163).

The differences in the novels' portrayal of landscape, in narrators' attitudes to the control of technology, and in the portrayal of relations of groups and individuals are directly tied, then, to the specific type of utopia advocated by the prophet-figure in each work.

The conflicts in California's garden take place not only at the level of physical confrontation or violence, moreover, but also at the level of ideas. If the parody of Canaan that is California in the novels' rural/agricultural settings is to be transformed according to a vision of utopia, then some form of cooperative or supportive behavior will have to supplant the ideology that sponsors the predatory behavior of the large landowners.

From one point of view, the utopia of *Parched Earth* seems to be confirmed. Dave Washburn and other members of the Caldwell proletariat help one another to safety as the flood accidentally unleashed by Wally, the capitalist's offspring, figuratively foreshadows the coming of the proletarian revolution. "History was made," the narrator comments, as the waters engulf a home where a mother and daughter are discussing the American Revolution of 1776 (408). Like a latter-day Noah, Washburn leads his little band to deliverance from wholesale destruction—not of course through divine intervention, but with the help of the group's own mutually supportive efforts. The narrator is decidedly vague, though, about the possible developments by which a proletarian revolution in the Tontos Valley (or anywhere else, for that matter), might be arrived at in practical political terms. Whether the figurative triumph is a satisfactory substitute for such a political design is doubtful.

In some ways, the claim for the likelihood of major social change in *The Grapes of Wrath* is more explicitly ambitious: "They's gonna come somepin outa all these folks goin' wes' . . . that's gonna change the whole country" (190). It is true that in the short term the prospects for the triumph of Casy's utopia do not seem very hopeful. Casy himself is killed, and it is not made clear whether the strike he leads succeeds or not. On the other hand, Tom Joad consciously and deliberately takes up Casy's mission after Casy's death, as in a sense Ma Joad does by urging Rose of Sharon to breastfeed the starving migrant. Moreover Casy is only the spokesperson for a mass movement that is presented as having a life and a momentum of its own.[22] If John Ditsky, when he comments that the Joads will have to find "a Canaan within, or not at all" at the end of their exodus from Oklahoma, alludes to their failure to find economic abundance he is obviously right;[23] but Casy's preaching of a utopia of community and mutuality points forward to the possibility of future radical change in that system.

As for the applicability of William Propter's utopia to society at large, the prophet-figure himself makes clear that such a development is highly improbable. His marginal social experiment, however, enjoys a limited success. To be sure, his most promising disciple, Pete Boone, is murdered by Jo Stoyte, but Propter will carry on the work he has begun with his little community.

At the close of *Co-op*, the fate of the cooperative utopia organized by Charlie Day and Sigvald Soren is left in the balance. The Self-Help Exchange is presented as at least potentially successful. After two years the seven hundred members of the Self-Help Exchange are able to acquire forty percent of their daily needs through work for the cooperative (305). Moreover, Sigvald Soren claims that the American people are taking up the organization of cooperatives nationwide. The EPIC program attracts voter support away from the traditional parties (220). Yet the members of the Self-Help Exchange continue in "slow starvation" because of governmental indifference or obstruction (385). For Sinclair's narrator, the real obstacle to the success of the cooperative utopia seems to be not San Sebastian's capitalists who are practical enough to recognize a workable program and support it, if it does not threaten their immediate interests, but rather the federal government, whose bureaucratic meddling discredits the cooperative movement through the founding of unworkable "cooperative schemes" and takes the best workers in the San Sebastian Self-Help Exchange to earn their welfare money on futile WPA projects (385, 330). Ultimately, the fate of Sinclair's cooperative utopia is presented as dependent upon the willingness of the Roosevelt administration to support it (415).[24]

Quite aside from the degree of success one is led to infer for the utopias preached by the prophet-figures, in each case at least the conditions for preaching of a utopia are created. The first and essential condition is disillusionment—a perception of disparity between a California of deprivation and hunger, and the vision of California as Canaan or Eden, a land of abundance of which the California of deprivation and hunger is a parody. Given the role played in the creation of this parody by predatory greed, it is not surprising that in each of the four novels the vision of utopia involves a movement beyond the original conception of self-centered enjoyment and aggrandizement to some form of cooperation and identification with others. This is the common ground shared by the otherwise very different utopias of Armstrong, Steinbeck, Huxley and Sinclair. The second condition seems to be the existence of the rural/agricultural setting itself. While economic exploitation has made of it a parody of the Promised Land, California's garden remains an appropriate site for the communication of utopian messages. The context of organic growth and natural abundance is presented as being, both literally and figuratively speaking, fertile ground. This is a condition which invites contrast with the unfertile setting of California's "natural museum," where the prophet-figures preach in vain.

Notes

1 These biblical resonances in turn lend authority to the prophet figures, who themselves parody biblical originals.

2 For W. Richard Fossey, writing in the *Cimarron Review* in 1973, *The Grapes of Wrath* is also "an epic of disillusionment with the Western dream" (33). Bernard Bowron made a similar, more detailed case nineteen years earlier, in "*The Grapes of Wrath*: A 'Wagons West' Romance." As Bowron points out, one element in the effect of the novel's closing chapters as experienced by many readers is the realization that the West is not to be "won"—or not as it is won in the traditional Western movie. Hence, "The fate of these 'modern pioneers' is felt as utterly outrageous, precisely because it outrages the genre ending" (91).

3 See Hicks' review of *The Grapes of Wrath*, reprinted in Robbins.

4 Marshal V. Hartranft's *Grapes of Gladness: California's Refreshing and Inspiring Answer to John Steinbeck's 'The Grapes of Wrath'* persisted in endorsing this view: "If everybody knew how to take a living direct from the resources of the earth like the California Indians did, we would never hear anything about want or hunger" (135). Reprinted in French, *Casebook*.

5 As H. Kelly Crockett pointed out in his 1962 essay, "The Bible and *The Grapes of Wrath*," grapes in both the Old and New Testament function as a "biblical symbol of fruitfulness, renewal and of promise" (194). Crockett reminds the reader that the first sign to the Israelites in the Wilderness that Canaan would be a fruitful land was a bunch of grapes (195). Thus the description of the putrefaction of the grapes in *The Grapes of Wrath* suggests the decay of the promise of the Promised Land.

6 Besides being a prophet-figure who, like the prophet-figures of *Parched Earth* and *The Grapes of Wrath*, addresses the specific issues raised by the needs of migrant workers in Depression-era California, Propter belongs to a line of religious teacher or preacher figures in other Huxley novels. Miller, in *Eyeless in Gaza* (1936), is a character partly modeled on Huxley's friend and mentor Gerald Heard. Miller and Propter were to be followed by Bruno Rontini (*Time Must Have a Stop*, 1945), and Rivers (*The Genius and the Goddess*, 1955).

7 For Leo Marx the question addressed in nineteenth-century American literature was that of the invasion of the garden by the machine, of the machine's "increasing domination of the visible world." These changes in turn meant for the American writer, according to Marx, that the pastoral idyll which in

literature embodies "an inspiriting vision of a humane community" was largely rendered obsolete; and that new metaphors for the vision of utopia would have to be found (364). *Parched Earth*, *The Grapes of Wrath*, *After Many a Summer* and *Co-op* all retain the pre-industrial, rural idyll to varying degrees, but suggest that the threat to their respective utopias in the agrarian setting is not the machine per se, but rather exclusive control of the machine by a few.

8 The wreck of a train as a metaphor for the catastrophic demise of American capitalism is also used in a fictional sketch by Mike Gold, in which "America is a private train rushing to Hollywood" (Folsom 147).

9 Fontenrose has remarked on Steinbeck's apparent confusion about the notion of economic success as a measure of human successfulness in general (95). Steinbeck's attitude to the small capitalist—to the farmer or storekeeper or restaurant owner—is generally favorable. It is the tycoon or the "faceless" corporate executive whom Steinbeck's narrator in *The Grapes of Wrath* treats as dehumanized by economic success and therefore lacking in sensitivity to the needs of others.

10 "Railroads build themselves," Shelgrim tells Presley when the latter confronts him with the misery wrought by the entry of the railroad into the economy of California's wheat region. "Where there is a demand, sooner or later there will be a supply" (285). Although Annette Kolodny, in *The Lay of the Land*, discusses a number of twentieth-century works, she undertakes no discussion of *The Grapes of Wrath*. This omission seems surprising, given her project for seeking "a radically mythic new symbolic mode" for relating to the idea of America. "We can no longer afford to keep turning America the Beautiful into America the Raped," she writes (148). The description of the tractors in Chapter Five of *The Grapes of Wrath* contains, after all, one of the best-known images of the rape of the land in all North American literature. One might venture to suggest that Kolodny's project for de-mythifying the idea of the rape of America's land would be fatally altered if it took into account such questions as whether "rape" in an ecological sense continues to take place—and whether the question of human ownership of land and technology needs to be addressed before any reshaping of the "myth" toward political/social ends is a possibility.

11 Whether or not the reader of *Civilizing the Machine* feels comfortable with John Kasson's all-inclusive, vaguely defined concept of republicanism, Kasson offers a reminder that nineteenth-century writers of utopian fiction like Edward Bellamy and William Dean Howells were preoccupied with the role of technology in American society.

12 Granville Hicks commended *Parched Earth* for its "truly Marxian" insight into "the action of social forces" (Robbins 77). Not all left-wing critics were so easily satisfied. Edwin Seaver, writing in *The New Republic*, criticized the novel's avoidance of depiction of any literal revolutionary dénouement to class conflict; Armstrong, Seaver complained, "permits a bursting dam to rob the workers of their historic role. . . . Why bring in communism and the need

for organization if we are to find salvation at the hands of a cretin and experience revolution by water?"

13 Critics have disagreed for five decades over the utopian vision allegedly projected by *The Grapes of Wrath*, and also over what elements of existing social ideology the novel contains, and in what proportion. Warren French is no doubt correct in his assertion that "Steinbeck is definitely not a collectivist," if by "collectivist" French means an advocate of large-scale, centrally bureaucratized collective farming as practiced in the U.S.S.R. Charles L. Sanford finds in *The Grapes of Wrath* a "Marxian class analysis," which yet "favors character transformation over revolution" (311). While, as will be argued in Chapter Five of this study, Steinbeck was actively engaged in debate and dialogue with the American Left, and entertained a certain respect—albeit mingled with suspicion—for some of its rank-and-file organizers; and while a dialectical conflict of social forces is clearly traceable in *The Grapes of Wrath*, to describe Steinbeck's analysis as "Marxian" is to overstate the case. There is certainly nothing marxian about the solution he advocates to the plight of the migrants—enabling them to become small-holders. Chester Eisinger, like Frederic Carpenter, plausibly identifies the narrator of *The Grapes of Wrath* as an advocate of "the agrarianism of Jefferson," in which individual tenure by small landowners is seen as the guarantee of political democracy (149). For Richard Astro, Steinbeck's approach to his fiction, including *The Grapes of Wrath*, is formulated less in terms of traditional political or economic categories than in terms of "ecology," in the sense of an awareness of the interrelatedness of natural phenomena. For Stoddard Martin "socialistic sympathies . . . scream out of" *The Grapes of Wrath* (74), while John Ditsky reads the novel not as "a call to revolutionary action" but rather as "a clear warning to middle-class readers" of the danger of class warfare in California if the grievances of the migrants continue to be ignored (217). Stanley Edgar Hyman in 1942 expressed a similar view; the novel, he wrote, was to be understood as "an appeal to the owning class to behave" rather than as a call to the dispossessed to revolt (195). These interpretations obviously rule out the possibility that the novel projects a utopia for which a precondition would be seizure of the means of production by the propertyless. There does seem little doubt, however, that sharing and working of land is part of the utopian vision of *The Grapes of Wrath*. Perhaps Joseph Fontenrose is closest to the mark when he writes of the Steinbeckian utopia adumbrated in *The Grapes of Wrath* as one of "a cooperative society based on small landholdings" (96). (To refer as he does to such a utopia as "Chestertonian Distributivism," however, serves only to confuse the issue.)

14 Aldous Huxley wrote to Julian about his plans for *After Many a Summer*: "I'm working on a novel and collecting whatever information I can pick up in regard to the technique for giving a viable economic and social basis to philosophic anarchism" (*Letters* 434).

15 For the significance of the image of the mountain in Huxley's fiction, see *Those Barren Leaves*, in which a character who has chosen the life of a hermit seeks transcendental meaning in contemplation of a mountain landscape: "Beautiful, terrible and mysterious, pregnant with what enormous secret,

symbolic of what formidable reality?" (116). For Huxley writing in 1962 the experience of space and distance is "the first and fundamental religious experience" (*Island* 183).

16 Huxley had long argued against the possibility of radically transforming society at the center, and was particularly distrustful of the consequences of social change brought about by violence. In *Ends and Means* (1937) he contends that "Means determine ends. Violence and coercion produce a post-revolutionary society, not communistic but (like the Russian) hierarchical, ruled by an oligarchy using secret police methods" (111).

17 In his 1962 utopian fiction *Island*, Huxley was to depict a complete society organized along lines similar to those his character Propter advocates for the few in *After Many a Summer*. The author's underlying pessimism about the actual viability of his ideals, even for a small, isolated island community, is indicated, however, by the novel's conclusion, in which a military invasion from the mainland destroys utopia. What remains, in *Island*, is the ever-present possibility of self-transcendence for the individual.

18 Benson records the labor organizing philosophy of Pat Chambers, whom he interviewed. "The essence of leadership," Chambers told Benson, admittedly many years after his involvement in the California migrant strikes of the 1930s, "Is not to portray yourself as some sort of know-it-all, but your ability to develop the people you are working with so they themselves can take the initiative" (300). According to Benson, Chambers was critical of the portrayal of farm labor organizers as cynical, devious manipulators in *In Dubious Battle*. Organizers did not need the elaborate subterfuges resorted to by Jim and Mac in order to make contact with workers, Chambers claimed. All that was necessary, he told Benson, was "to slip into camp and put up a union sign someplace" (300, 304).

19 The phalanx of *In Dubious Battle* is a bloodthirsty creature. The mere sight of blood is apparently capable of stirring it to action, as in the scene where a violent fight moves a crowd of strikers to go out and tear down a vigilante barricade (315). In *The Grapes of Wrath* more benign aspects of phalanx behavior are depicted. The migrant phalanx is primarily viewed as a support system—the twenty families becoming one—although always with the underlying threat of collective armed rebellion. Actual violence in the novel is committed by individuals, and of course by the "phalanx" of the big landowners, represented by the banks, the land companies and by the mob madness of the vigilantes who set fire to the Hoovervilles (309-10).

20 Mac himself later realizes that the strike leaders can direct the actions of the strikers' phalanx only to a very limited extent: "It's swell when we can use it, but we don't know enough. When it gets started it might do anything" (317).

21 In a letter written in 1933 Steinbeck made a dramatic statement of his faith in the autonomous capabilities of the phalanx: "It can alter the birth rate, diminish the number of its units, control states of mind, alter appearance, physically and spiritually . . ." (*Letters* 75). In the light of this faith one may doubt the usefulness of Frederic I. Carpenter's 1941 formulation of the rela-

tionship between prophet-figure and society in *The Grapes of Wrath*. According to Carpenter, "Jim Casy's ideas determine and direct the Joads' actions" (315). Closer examination of the incidents in the novel where Tom is shown meditating the possibility of strike action long before Casy's own involvement (271) or where Ma Joad offers her own formulation of the concept of the Oversoul (230), show Carpenter's statement to be only partially accurate.

22 Stanley Trachtenberg's assessment of this question seems to me to exaggerate the pessimism of *The Grapes of Wrath*. Nothing in the novel, according to Trachtenberg, "promises any extended alleviation of human misery. . . . Loss is attended solely by the consolation of despair" (7). To make this statement with any degree of credibility Trachtenberg has to overemphasize Tom Joad's "marginality" to society, and to dismiss the breast-giving scene at the close of the novel as "irrelevant" to the social concerns it addresses elsewhere.

23 "The Joads will have to learn to find their Canaan in their inner selves or not at all" (216).

24 To Sinclair's frustration, Roosevelt who (Sinclair claimed) had personally promised to speak publicly in favor of EPIC refrained from committing himself on the matter (McIntosh 169).

Chapter Three

On Fertile Ground

In *The Lay of The Land* (1975) Annette Kolodny noted a centuries-old impulse among writers describing North America to view the country's rural landscape in terms of "the female principle of gratification." It is an impulse which the description in *The Grapes of Wrath* of fruitful orchard slopes "round and soft as breasts" clearly exemplifies (382). For the most part, however, in *The Grapes of Wrath*, as in *Parched Earth*, *After Many a Summer* and *Co-op*, the fruitfulness of the earth as mother is wasted through human greed. It may further be argued that human fruitfulness—that of women as potential wives and mothers—is similarly wasted. The primarily rural/agricultural settings of *The Grapes of Wrath*, of *Parched Earth*, and of *Co-op* invite the drawing of analogies between the defeated expectations of the land as nurturing and fruitful and the failure of women to nurture and bear fruit. They also suggest a correlation between the "fruitfulness" of women characters and the success of fictional prophet-figures' utopias. All three novels rely heavily, in fact, on stereotypes of women as, like the land, ideally fulfilled through biological fertility.

In *The Grapes of Wrath*, *Parched Earth* and *Co-op*, women parody an original fruitful "Earth-Mother," in the sense that they present an ironic contrast with this original. Those women in *The Grapes of Wrath* and *Parched Earth* who for different reasons are forced to be "barren" are, by their failure in motherhood, presented as parodies of this patriarchally-conditioned ideal of womanhood.

After Many a Summer and *The Day of the Locust*, located as they are in what Randall Reid has called the "natural museum" setting of Hollywood and Southern California, offer examples of women who deviate from the patriarchal ideal of fruitful womanhood by their casual promiscuity. The settings in which the women of these novels move are "artificial" in the sense that they are exaggerated human contrivances, constructed from inorganic materials, and also that they in turn function as parodies of other settings. (This point will be dealt with at length in Chapter Four.) In the settings of a tycoon's castle or of a Hollywood suburb, women are made over into consumers, or consumer objects, or both. Like the women in *Parched Earth*, *The Grapes of Wrath*, or *Co-op* the women in the natural museum settings are parodies of the fulfilled wife-and-mother ideal.

Childlessness, the sickness or loss of a child and the connotations of sterility and death which that lack or loss carry with them, are closely associated in all five novels with the destructive effects of the California Dream and the predatory individualism which the Dream fosters. Given a society in which the roles of men and women are rigidly demarcated, with a heavy emphasis on the female's domestic and childbearing functions, and given the challenges posed to that society by the breakdown of these traditional roles in the wholesale loss of employment and land tenure brought about by the Depression, it is hardly surprising that fulfillment or unfulfillment of the traditional female role should be a major preoccupation of a number of Depression-era writers. Childlessness and child sickness and death serve as indicators of a social malaise affecting the culture and, in the novelists' presentations, the future of that culture. The degree to which women overcome their childless condition is, to some extent, coterminous with the success of the prophet-figure in each of the five novels in communicating his vision of utopia and offering the hope of a new future for those identifying with it.

The novels of the "natural museum" setting differ markedly from those with primarily rural/ agricultural settings in their presentation of female characters who evince no desire for marriage, pregnancy or domesticity. This choice is implicitly or explicitly condemned by the narrators. Childless, unmarried women in *After Many a Summer* and *The Day of the Locust* are presented as social parasites and victims of their compulsive sexual desires. The "artificial" setting they inhabit is presented as having "distorted" their behavior, making the attainment of wifehood and motherhood impossible.

In both *After Many a Summer* and *The Day of the Locust* a promiscuous, childless female figure is presented as a destructive and morally culpable influence; yet her destructive effects on others are symptomatic of a social malaise which extends well beyond the agency and moral responsibility of a single individual. The infidelity of Huxley's Virginia Maunciple leads to the killing of an innocent; but the murder of Pete Boone is also brought about by the uncontrolled possessiveness of her lover-benefactor, the tycoon Jo Stoyte, and the unscrupulous experimental curiosity of Virginia's other lover, Obispo. The tragedy is a consequence of a whole complex of unrestrained human fears and cravings, in which Virginia's promiscuity is only one factor. In *The Day of the Locust* Faye Greener is a victim of economic exploitation as well as a victimizer and parasite on others. To some extent, at least, she is a dupe of the Hollywood version of the California Dream. The collective violence which erupts at the novel's close is the product of a destructive rage in which everyone, including Tod Hackett, the novel's prophet-figure, is complicit.

Social malaise is suggested in both novels through the use of images of children, who for the most part are connected with thwarted desires, destructiveness or actual death. In *After Many a Summer* the central female figure is childless and repelled by the idea of pregnancy. We are reminded, too, that the late wife of the predatory tycoon Jo Stoyte, who has been responsible for much human suffering, was biologically unable to bear children. The children of the novel's representative migrant worker, the man from Kansas, are sickly and liable to contract hookworm from their unsanitary living conditions on Jo Stoyte's estate (40, 265). (Ironically, Stoyte funds a hospital for sick children whose doors are usually closed to the children of the migrants). Children playing under the walls of the Stoyte castle serve as reminders to the reader of the concurrent deaths of other children in the war in China (230). In a description of a mother ape's pathetic compulsion to groom the dead baby she refuses to abandon, the motif is repeated in the context of the animal kingdom.

Although the image of the ape mother recalls Huxley's rejection of the world of "appearance," his insistence that biological ties and desires are a trap and delusion, the death and sickness of human children in *After Many a Summer* as a direct consequence of exploitation or war, are crucial in indicating the economic and moral failures of a particular society. If the fictional world of *After*

Many a Summer is the world of appearance, time and evil from the perspective of Huxley's metaphysical schema, it is also the world of predatory greed in which William Propter's gospel of community is the exception rather than the rule—in which Jo Stoyte in his exploitation of his migrant employees and Obispo in his speculation in wartime aircraft shares stand as representative of those predators who profit from violence done to others.

The Day of the Locust shares with *After Many a Summer* a use of images of childlessness and of the frustration or redirection of maternal impulses. Most characters of either sex in *The Day of the Locust* have no children. A number of them—Homer Simpson, Earle Shoop, Miguel, Abe Kusich, the prophet-figure Tod Hackett—are solitary, rootless drifters, without any claim to a "family life" at all. A number of the female characters redirect maternal impulses in unusual ways. Mrs. Johnson, the janitress at Tod Hackett's lodging, parodies maternal behavior in her authoritative managing of other people's lives and the arrangement of their funerals. This latter service she renders "selflessly" in the spirit of an authoritarian parent who knows what is good for her children. "I don't get anything out of it, and it's just a lot of trouble," she claims (123). Audrey Jennings, the Hollywood actress turned brothelkeeper for whom Faye Greener works, displays a similar attitude to her employees, on whose behalf she investigates the background of prospective customers (73). The one biological mother dealt with at any length in *The Day of the Locust* is a Hollywood mother, "one of that army of women who drag their children from casting office to casting office . . . waiting for a chance to show what Junior can do" (138). In this instance it is her child Adore who in his disquietingly precocious sophistication parodies the innocence and spontaneity of childhood. Adore is on the one hand a small automaton who performs sexually suggestive material when goaded by his mother, on the other a potential juvenile delinquent who snarls at strangers when her back is turned.[1] Mrs. Loomis, the mother, presents one more instance of the operation of predatory self-interest, which has succeeded in turning her child into "the Frankenstein Monster" (147). The only other parent whose relationship with his child is depicted in detail is the father of the parasitic, predatory Faye Greener.[2]

While images of childhood perform an important function in *After Many a Summer* and *The Day of the Locust* as suggestive registers of social malaise, the centrality of parodies of the woman as wife and mother makes the main female characters of crucial importance. Huxley's Virginia Maunciple, like a number of characters in Huxley's earlier work, was a model for West, and Huxley himself a literary mentor.[3] Moreover, Virginia, in her explicit revulsion at the ideas of pregnancy and domesticity, offers an unambiguous example of parodic deviation from the ideals of monogamy and maternity, a significance recognized at least to some extent by the character herself.[4] West's Faye Greener, on the other hand, in her attachment to Hollywood's values and to a version of the California Dream which for her involves the pursuit of stardom regardless of the human cost, appears able to justify to herself her pursuit of sexual relations and her parasitism upon men for material goods without thought of emotional commitment. Huxley's Virginia Maunciple, however, still largely endorses the patriarchal ideal of womanhood she betrays, and feels guilty about her betrayal of her lover and benefactor Jo Stoyte with another man. Her devotion to the Virgin Mary, to whom she guiltily confesses her infidelities, is part of a sentimentally conventional world-view, of which motherhood would probably be a part if she could overcome her revulsion at the idea of pregnancy. In her maternal solicitude for Jo Stoyte there is indeed, as Obispo, Virginia's lover reflects, something of the "Gold Star Mother" (138). Faye at her most enticing is incapable of evoking such an association. Her sexual appeal is "closer to murder than to love" (68).

Virginia Maunciple is only one of Huxley's portraits in *After Many a Summer* of individuals enslaved to their sexuality and hence, in Huxley's terms, to the world of "time and appearance."[5] The novel portrays calculating, manipulative sadism (Obispo), romantic idealism (Pete Boone), infantile self-gratification (Jeremy Pordage), possessive dependency (Jo Stoyte). Compared with such a collection of aberrations, Virginia's unreflecting spontaneous sensuality might be regarded as less unattractive—even attractive. Her aversion to the idea of maternity is, however, presented as indicative of a psychological inadequacy, a squeamishness with regard to female biology which the narrator satirizes and censures.

A statue of a female figure that spouts water from its breasts disgusts her (88). Her first shocked reaction to a reading of de Sade is that the offending passages are "Horrible! As bad as having babies" (169). Virginia's childlessness and fear of child-bearing represent a disorientation inextricably bound up with the "artificial" existence she leads as Stoyte's mistress and with her own role as Stoyte's parasite—his "baby."

In many respects Virginia is presented as being almost a child herself, who, although in her early twenties, gives the impression of being an adolescent. Her emotional immaturity is exemplified by her religious beliefs and practices, centered as they are around a "sacred doll's house" of the shrine of a virgin mother who apparently shares the worshipper's taste for personal adornment, being decked in "the cutest little gold crown" and "six strings of seed pearls" (176). It is apparent, too, in Virginia's naive narcissism: "Every victory for the Queen of Heaven was also a personal success for Virginia Maunciple" (88).

The rather obvious sexist joke of Virginia's name suggests that, although no virgin, she is an insulated child, ignorant about the functioning of her society. Her childish religious fantasies and her dependence on Jo Stoyte enable her to exist self-absorbedly, in a "mindless eternity" of present satisfactions which cuts her off from the possibility of relating to others (47). To her the migrant workers on Jo Stoyte's estate—to whom Propter will make himself a friend and a mentor—are remote "ant-like" figures. She wonders "idly" about the reason for their arrival, then finds her attention drawn to "more interesting and personal matters" (49).

Parasitic upon Stoyte, Virginia is his "baby" both literally and figuratively (45).[6] His castle is a womb in which she absorbs from him both material and emotional sustenance. Unaware of and indifferent to the means by which Stoyte's wealth was accumulated, she does not question his predatory values, either. His wealth simply exists for her "as though it grew on trees—a swimming pool tree, a cocktail tree . . . you just had to reach out your hand" (47). Ironically, she has what the migrants of *The Grapes of Wrath* dreamed of before their arrival in California—a private orchard offering unlimited abundance.

Virginia's emotional recoil from the idea of pregnancy cannot be considered in isolation from what her world has made of her. A vulnerable innocence which shades readily into naiveté about her own motives, and thence into self-deception and behavior which threatens the well-being of others, seems to have functioned as a mode of survival in the sleazy milieu of the night-club dancer, where she found herself vulnerable to "some fellow taking advantage of her being so dumb and innocent" with "nothing on but a G-string and some talcum powder" (186). Virginia's lack of control over her sexual appetites continues—at least until Obispo robs her of some of her illusions—to be justified by self-deception. She likes to be seduced "almost without . . . knowing it, almost as if it weren't happening" (178). She views her two lesbian relationships retrospectively as "a kind of little accident; nice, but not a bit important." These memories typify the casual relationships into which Virginia passively drifts—and perhaps, in her insistence that these liaisons were both "nice" and unimportant, the degree to which her unawareness of her own motives makes her the vulnerable object of others' designs and desires. The two relationships are, in terms of this narrative, presented as a further aspect of her failure to attain a "mature" sexuality in a world which rewards her for remaining a bewildered child, but at a high price.

Virginia is presented as maintaining a simple-minded goodwill in dealing with her social world: "She liked to like people . . . she liked to please them" (46). Yet her easy acquiescence in sexual relationships leads to Pete Boone's death when the jealous Stoyte kills him after mistaking him as her lover. It leads to a new consciousness of guilt and self-disgust, as she continues to sleep with her lover, Obispo, who openly revels in his power over her (298).

The price in death and emotional suffering is paid for "promiscuity," and for rapacity, given the moral obtuseness it appears to have fostered in the predatory capitalist Stoyte and in its beneficiary, Virginia. Given the author's strongly moralistic bent and the specific dictum of the novel's prophet-figure William Propter, "God is not mocked," the novel is susceptible of both these readings. Furthermore, Virginia's "sterility," her revulsion from reproduction, is a suggestive metaphor for "sterile" conditions fostered by the Dream in the victims of the Dream. Through a figurative transference which is not without connotations of "blaming the victim," the reader may conclude that Virginia's unfruitfulness is also a key agent of destructiveness in the novel.

In West's *The Day of the Locust*, promiscuity, sterility, predatory individualism and death are presented as interrelated. The childless woman who serves as the focus in this nexus of ideas in *The Day of the Locust* is Faye Greener. Like Virginia Mauncipe she is both promiscuous and childless. Moreover, she too is driven by predatory instincts, and she too arouses a death-wish in others.

At seventeen, Faye is in many ways a precocious adolescent who consciously and unconsciously combines childish traits—her unabashedly greedy appetite,[7] her affectation of sailor collars, hair ribbons and brightly colored sandals—with an adult sophistication (94).

Although much younger than Virginia, Faye shows greater self-reflexivity. At times she is fully aware that her affected mannerisms and her fantasies of stardom are equally absurd. Tod Hackett has seen her actually "laugh at her dreams" (104). Her very artificiality is more calculated than that of Virginia. Her dress and demeanor at her father's funeral, for example, in a "very tight" black dress are a carefully contrived blend of funereal propriety and sexual allure: "Ever so often, she carried a tiny lace handkerchief to her eyes and made it flutter there for a moment" (126). To her parodies of the bereaved dutiful daughter, the unaffected child, the sophisticated Hollywood actress, Faye brings a calculation and detachment which afford her an advantage over those other followers of the California Dream, Tod and Homer, for example, whom she exploits.

Like Virginia, Faye lives a good deal of the time in a fantasy world formed of the images and desires of a consumer society in which sexual experience (Virginia calls it "yum-yum") is one more object of consumption. For Faye these fantasies primarily take the form of the movie-script daydreams which at times possess her: "She seemed always to be struggling in their soft grasp as if she were trying to run in a swamp" (106-7). For all her calculating intelligence, she, like her victims, is one of "The Cheated" (as West had originally intended to title his novel). She too yields herself, wittingly and willingly, to the power of the Dream.

Like Virginia, Faye is parasitic on men for material support—again, more calculatingly so: "She wasn't sentimental and she had no need for tenderness" (68). She lives with Homer, whom she baits and despises, because although she prefers Tod, Tod "couldn't further her career." If she rejects other than good-looking men, she will "only let a wealthy man love her" (67).[8] If Faye chooses the host on whom to feed more consciously than Virginia does, like Virginia, nonetheless, she gives the appearance of straying without long-term calculation from one sexual involvement to another. Tod thinks of her at one point as being "like a cork" (173). If to Tod the analogy suggests chiefly her capacity for survival, it also suggests a helpless drifting before the changing winds and tides of circumstance.

As in the case of Virginia's affair with Obispo, Faye's sexual entanglements arouse destructive instincts in the males with whom she is involved. On the two occasions when she becomes the center of attraction of a gathering of men—once at Miguel's desert shack and once at Homer's house—a fight breaks out. Faye arouses both masochistic and sadistic impulses in Tod Hackett, who reflects that to love her would be "like throwing yourself from the parapet of a skyscraper" (68). On another occasion he tracks her as prey, "bellowing" like a hound "when it strikes a fresh line after hours of cold trailing" (117); or he fantasizes about pouncing on her and raping her (174). Faye herself is sadistic in baiting her sick father and humiliating Homer (122, 144).

Calculating, self-serving, parasitic and destructive, Faye is both victim and victimizer. This orphan daughter of a failed comedian survives by the use of her wits when the meager income of a film extra fails to support her. Yet, like Huxley's Virginia Maunciple, she is a product of a world in which to "succeed"—or even to survive—women are obliged to use their wits for the marketing of their bodies. Like the other frustrated citizens of Los Angeles depicted in Tod's painting of "The Burning of Los Angeles," Faye experiences the failure of her dreams to satisfy her. In the painting, where frustration is depicted as breaking out into violence, she is again portrayed as hunted prey, but also as enjoying the release of flight after pent-up inaction. She can transcend the influence of the California Dream no more than any of the other characters in *The Day of the Locust*. She is both symptom and agent of the general social malaise, and also portrayed as its victim.[9]

The centrality of the childless, promiscuous, parasitic woman to both *After Many a Summer* and *The Day of the Locust*—the inability of women to give birth, suckle or nurture—is an index of the prophet-figures' relative lack of success in countering the pervading influence of the California Dream or in communicating a vision of utopia. In *After Many a Summer* Virginia remains childless. Correspondingly she, like most of the inhabitants of Stoyte's castle (except Pete Boone, who is accidentally killed on the very day he adopts Propter's philosophy) remains completely unmoved by Propter's preaching. As for the migrants, the man from Kansas is presented as listening attentively to his preaching, yet the novel makes clear that for personal economic reasons as well as the broader social reasons outlined in Chapter Two, Propter's work has barely begun and is likely to be limited in its focus and marginal to his society as a whole. That Virginia remains a parody of the fulfilled wife and mother is wholly in keeping with the limited success of the prophet-figure, and his inability to communicate his message to the inhabitants of the "natural museum" setting. In *The Day of the Locust* Faye Greener alters even less than Virginia. Whereas the latter begins to experience guilt about her infidelity to Jo Stoyte and about her responsibility for the death of Pete Boone, to the novel's end Faye remains rootless and childless, and indifferent to the violence she arouses in others. Unlike Propter, Tod has no utopia to offer. His chiliastic message, presented in a painting, announces only a shared experience based on destruction—a mad rampage of "the people who come to California to die" (184).

By contrast with *After Many a Summer* and *The Day of the Locust*, *Parched Earth*, *The Grapes of Wrath* and *Co-op* are characterized by a partial redemption of the social malaise they portray, and the prophets' messages are more fully heeded and practiced. In all three of these novels with a rural/agricultural setting the land's abundance is wasted through human greed, but not without a hope of abundance restored in the future. The prophet-figures' qualified success in preaching their utopian programs is paralleled by the "cure" of "barrenness" or the fertility of a female character. The three novels differ in the type of utopia advocated by the prophet-figure: marxist-leninist in *Parched Earth*, New Deal liberal and Jeffersonian in *The Grapes of Wrath* (although not without an implied dialogue with more radical left-wing ideas), cooperative socialist in *Co-op*. They share, however, a common moral indignation about the wasteful or destructive practices of contemporary agricultural capitalism.

Parched Earth appeared five years earlier than *The Grapes of Wrath* and two years before *Co-op*. Unlike Steinbeck's novels, or Sinclair's, in its narration of the "cure" of a woman's barrenness it fulfills, rather than transcends, the norm of wifehood and motherhood of which Hattie Rathbone's barrenness and Belle Vasquez's bearing of an idiot son represent parodies. Consideration of the fulfillment of this norm in *Parched Earth* seems a logical step before moving on to consider the partial transcendence of the norm by Rose of Sharon in *The Grapes of Wrath* and by Maisie Trent and Mabel Saugus in *Co-op*.

In *Parched Earth*, as in *The Grapes of Wrath* and *Co-op*, California's fertility never fails; but the land's produce, its "offspring," is squandered by human greed; and *Parched Earth* and *Co-op* make an equally systematic use of the idea of women as victims. The victimizer in *Parched Earth* is the landowner Everett Caldwell who has monopolized the resources of the Tontos Valley and the town to which he has given his name. Both the town prostitute Belle Vasquez, descendent of the Spanish settlers of California, and the cannery worker Hattie Rathbone, descendent of Anglo-Saxon pioneers, have been forced off land their families once owned. Belle's son by Everett Caldwell has been mentally retarded from birth owing to his father's syphilis. With his disease-related handicap and his insatiable appetite for food, Wally serves as an image for the corruption and greed of Caldwell's world. He possesses a number of his father's vices—a total absorption in his own wants and cravings being the most obvious—but grotesquely parodied, and without his father's calculating intelligence. When he exposes his genitals to the shocked eyes of the local citizens he also, the reader is told, figuratively exposes the culpability of his father and his father's business associates. He reveals that the moral and material economy of Caldwell are based on "show and no foundation . . . started by thievery and kept up the same way" (115). The deformed and retarded Wally, not unlike Rose of Sharon's dead baby (which is sent out into the world as a rebuke to the unawareness of California citizens) represents a "skeleton in the closet that you can't lock the door on." Belle, and after Belle's suicide, Hattie, in assuming the burden (however reluctantly) of caring for Wally, represent an alternative to the selfishness and hypocrisy of Everett Caldwell, who has not only striven for years to conceal the fact of his parenthood, but has refused any responsibility for Wally's upkeep.

Unlike Belle, Hattie is childless, and believes herself unable to bear a child. Her barrenness serves as a suggestive avatar of the novel's title. The "parching" is not a consequence of climatic conditions but of economic ones, of Everett Caldwell's monopoly of Tontos Valley irrigation rights, and of the ruin of local farmers who cannot sell their fruit profitably at Caldwell's prices. As in *The Grapes of Wrath* the earth produces but its fruits are wasted, and women's productivity is blighted.

Hattie becomes a convert to the marxist utopia preached by Dave Washburn. After she and the other cannery workers are routed by Caldwell's thugs at the factory gates, she recalls the words of Hop Collins, Washburn's disciple, about the necessity of class struggle: ". . . stick and fight it out. You got to git together with yore fellow man" (149-50). After being tear-gassed by Caldwell's vigilantes she concludes, "Hop was right. . . . You had to fight!" (165).

Because Hattie, a member of the proletariat, consciously aligns herself with her class, her inability to satisfy her longing to have a child assumes a central importance within the novel's marxist schema. After her mother's death, Hattie considers suicide as a means of escape from her wretched loneliness. Unlike Belle Vasquez, the last descendent of the Valley's Spanish feudal landowners, however, Hattie does not kill herself but persuades the local barber Tod Strawn to sleep with her in order to have a child by him (326). The experiment is unsuccessful. Just as the monopoly capitalist Everett Caldwell can father only a mentally retarded child, portrayed as a monstrous emblem of Caldwell, so Tod, a member of the petty bourgeoisie, is unable to contribute to the engendering of future life. Only with the breaking of the pent-up waters from behind Everett Caldwell's dam, as "history is made" and a new world comes to birth,[10] does the novel close with the suggestion that Hattie will at last bear a child. In the very moment when the workers are communally engaged in helping one another to safety, the reader is told that Hattie carries a box of baby clothes "warm with the breath" of a "gurgling" baby (429).[11] Shortly before this collective escape to safety, Hattie has found her future husband in a fellow-worker, Hop Collins. He will be the father, socially and perhaps also biologically, of Hattie's child. In a world after the flood—and outside the time of the novel which predicts a marxist-leninist utopia—everyone will have work and access to the produce of a "rich harvest," and women too will be fruitful, as Dave Washburn's utopia of proletarian solidarity prevails.

The dissemination and acceptance of a program for a utopia is paralleled in *The Grapes of Wrath*, as in *Parched Earth*, by a corresponding move toward "mothering," a renewed capacity for nurturing, as for mutuality and community. The closing scene of *The Grapes of Wrath*, in which Rose of Sharon feeds the starving stranger, represents part of a pattern in which the capacity to nurture is a measure of prophet-figures' success in communicating their messages.[12] Rose of Sharon's action is spontaneous and unpremeditated.[13] Yet the changes in her character which make the action possible and have been prepared for throughout the novel represent only one strand of the presentation of an evolving "phalanx" of the novel's female characters.[14] As Warren Motley has convincingly demonstrated, *The Grapes of Wrath* owes a great deal to Robert Briffault's *The Mothers*, particularly in Steinbeck's portrayal of a shift from a patriarchal family structure to one led by a powerful woman, in which the daughters of the family come to play crucial roles, and in which community and nurturance are inextricably related.[15]

The development of the female phalanx in *The Grapes of Wrath* may be said to begin with the growth of Ma Joad's relationship with an outsider to the family, Sairy Wilson. Ma Joad accepts Sairy's gift of a quilt in which to wrap the dead Grampa for burial. Despite the proudly independent Joads' initial embarrassment, the outcome of such acts of mutual assistance is the sense of a "kin bond" (183). Later, as she nurses the dying Granma, Ma Joad tells her daughter that "dyin' is a piece of all dyin' and bearin' is a piece of all bearin' . . ." (230).

As Ma Joad adapts herself to new circumstances—"woman can change better'n a man" (467)— and by virtue of her endurance and flexibility assumes leadership of the Joad family, she develops a broader sense of community.[16] She tells the neighbor who helps

Rose of Sharon in labor, "Worse off we get, the more we got to do" (491).

Ma is in fact the first member of the Joad family to grasp the importance of thinking in terms of "we" in relation to the oppression of the landowners: "If we was all mad the same way . . . they wouldn't hunt nobody down" (83). Although it will fall to Tom as Casy's disciple to commit himself to involvement in collective action against the oppressor and on behalf of his community, Ma, in her feeding of a stranger's children,[17] has independently and instinctively acted in the spirit of Casy's preaching (284). Although puzzled by Tom's summary of Casy's gospel during the scene of their final parting, she lives it out in practice.

Ma communicates her intuitive understanding to Rose of Sharon, despite the daughter's initial insensitivity to others' needs.[18] The communication is not achieved without tensions. Even when Connie deserts Rose of Sharon, Ma is brusque in her exhortations to stoicism: "You git aholt on yaself. They's a lot of us here. . . . Come here now an' peel some potatoes" (296). The constant refrain of Ma's lectures is one of the need for the individual to mature beyond egocentricity to a bonding with the community.

There is no explicit evidence that Rose of Sharon is particularly influenced by Ma's homilies. Yet even before the loss of her baby, a change in character is discernible. Instead of "candying" herself, she shows a new independence and determination, insisting (against Ma's wise advice) on helping the family pick cotton in preference to sulking in resentment of Al's engagement to Aggie. The culmination of her new awareness of others' needs is her decision to breast-feed the starving man. Her "yes" to a stranger's need invokes the spirit of Casy's gospel.

As Warren Motley has suggested, the utopia of community in *The Grapes of Wrath* is a very fragile entity.[19] Its fragility is indicated not only by the precarious situation of the outlawed Tom Joad but in the evident ease with which a new workforce is found to break the strike at Pixley. Yet the series of gestures the novel depicts—the sharing of a tent, car, blanket, food; a jail protest and a strike; Tom's decision to follow Casy—all point to the possibility of a broader extension of the utopia of community and mutual support. Rose of Sharon's gesture further ratifies the successes of

Casy's preaching. In the act of suckling—an act of almost sacred importance in Steinbeck's fiction[20]—Rose of Sharon allows the starving stranger to assume the place of her dead child.

Of all the positive and generous actions depicted in *The Grapes of Wrath* the climax is surely the novel's closing incident of Rose of Sharon's gift of her mother's milk to a stranger. Like Hattie Rathbone, she finds fulfillment in the act of nurturing, smiling "mysteriously" as she cradles the man's head in her arms (502). In this act, Rose of Sharon in one sense remains within the cultural norm of woman fulfilled through nurturing, which in her childless state she parodied. In another she moves beyond it, since the recipient of her care is not her own child but an adult stranger, and since she and her mother assume the initiative for an action which flouts patriarchally-sanctioned norms of female behavior.[21]

Upton Sinclair's *Co-op* focuses attention on three female characters: the Louisiana migrant, Mel Jett; the Socialist benefactor of the San Sebastian cooperative, Mabel Saugus; and the wealthy young runaway, Maisie Trent, who eventually joins the Self-Help Exchange.

Mel Jett, wife of the novel's representative migrant worker, is (like Steinbeck's Rose of Sharon) already pregnant when the Jett family arrive in California. Like the other evicted and landless family members, Mel is described as "gaunt and pale" with hunger. She is "a sad-eyed, weary woman" (92). But, when she goes into labor on California soil, she, unlike Rose of Sharon, gives birth to a healthy child. The birth takes place in the main offices of the San Sebastian Self-Help Exchange, and the "midwives" for the delivery are the cooperative's female members, who board and feed the other Jett children. After the successful delivery (at which the late-arriving doctor performs little more than an adjunct role), the whole Jett family joins the Self-Help Exchange. The migrant child's birth in the cooperative thus represents, both figuratively and literally, the "birth" of cooperation among the citizens of San Sebastian.

A newspaper photograph of the event shows the Jetts with the new baby, and "a score or more members of the co-op as a background." In the narrator's words, "It was exactly like a scene from grand opera, where all the blacksmiths at the forge or all the peasants in the field cease their work and stand in a row and sing"

(113). A further analogy suggested by this grouping might be that of a nativity play—also an image of the mutual giving and nurturing surrounding a birth. The Jett child receives no visit from the Magi, but the news of his birth inspires the townspeople to shower his family with gifts (115). The analogy with the nativity is made explicit in Cristy Jett's ballad about the event. The ballad evokes that "stable manger" in "Bethlehem far away" where "a babe was born in the hay," then recounts how "Once in a personnel office" in California, "A babe on the floor did lay." The ballad's final verses celebrate the cooperative, where the members have learned "the better way" of social cooperation: "We chop the wood/For brotherhood/In Californy-ay!" If others will learn this lesson of "brotherhood" symbolized by the nativity, the ballad concludes, "The masters no more/Shall bleed the poor" (339-40). In bringing her newborn child into membership of the cooperative, Mel Jett figuratively represents the birth of a social utopia, and herself literally achieves "deliverance" from the status of a social victim.

Unlike Mel Jett, Mabel Saugus is a beneficiary, not a victim, of the existing social order. She lives on inherited wealth. However, like Mel, her pregnancy is figuratively associated with the success of the Self-Help Exchange. Through her work for the Exchange, she meets and marries Herbert Alding, a New Deal bureaucrat who plans with her for the success of the cooperative utopia. (Arguably, the marriage represents that union of California grass-roots utopian socialism with the administrative powers of the federal government, which the author of *Co-op* hoped to see fostered by the Roosevelt administration.)

Physically pregnant, uniting the cooperative members in good-will toward her, Mabel Saugus is also the parent, with Herbert Alding, of a figurative "child," their proposal for federal support of California cooperatives (331-32, 348). She thus escapes the parodic status of "old maid," into a new fertility, intellectual and physical.

Maisie Trent narrowly escapes becoming a parody of the wife/mother ideal of womanhood. The adventure which brings her to the Self-Help Exchange, her rescue from kidnaping into prostitution, represents both the victimization of women by men, and the commodification of female sexuality. Maisie Trent, rescued from the life of a Belle Vasquez, instead becomes the wife of the prophet-figure Sigvald Soren, and another productive member of the cooperative.

In the interest of dramatizing a sense of economic social and/or political crisis, the women in the novels are presented as various versions of parody of the patriarchally-constructed ideal of the woman as wife and mother. The narrator's comment on Ma Joad in *The Grapes of Wrath*, "If she swayed the family shook . . . ," if "society" were substituted for "family," would suggest the sources of these parodic presentations. They cannot be understood without reference to their sociohistorical and socioeconomic context,[22] to a world of largely stable patriarchal structures and patriarchal attitudes subjected to challenge by widespread male loss of economic power. From the perspective of the fictional California prophet-figures—or at least of the narrators who present them—the childlessness of some women and the destructiveness of others, the presence of child sickness and death, are phenomena consistent with the dispossession of tenants, the oppression of workers, the greed of capitalists, the destruction of cities and of Hoovervilles. They are a sign that the day of judgment is at hand.

The parodies are diverse, however. Characters in the three novels with a primarily rural/agricultural setting are for the most part shown simply as having, for various reasons, failed to be earth-mothers. Characters in novels with a "natural museum" setting, on the other hand, tend, not surprisingly, both to evoke the patriarchal norm of fulfilled wife and mother by its very absence, and to draw upon stereotypes available in Hollywood: the "dumb blonde," the *femme fatale*, the destructively possessive mother. *Parched Earth* and *The Grapes of Wrath* exhibit more diversity, but always with implied contrast with the wife-and-mother ideal.

Huxley's Virginia Maunciple, the former showgirl and millionaire's mistress, is an example of the "dumb blonde," simple-minded and sexually attractive. (Virginia is, of course, modeled on Marion Davies, the mistress of William Randolph Hearst, just as the Stoyte castle is modeled on Hearst's San Simeon.) Virginia makes her way in life not by calculated assessment of situations but by pleasing others through acquiescence in their fantasies about her. To Stoyte she is a "baby," to Obispo a cooperative subject in a psychosexual experiment, to Pete Boone a Pure Woman, the distant object of a hopelessly romantic love. Her variously projected meanings to others make her an easy prey of any self-interested individualist. The implied moral judgment upon her is that she does not mind being thus victimized, that her meaning is a function of others' projections, and of their designs upon her.

Faye Greener, although she shares Virginia's passivity before changing circumstances, lacks Virginia's acquiescent attitude to other people's demands upon her, and remains for the most part stubbornly self-contained, protected by her "egg-like" self-sufficiency. She is a type of *femme fatale*, a siren who destroys the men she fascinates; but she is also an unrealistically ambitious and economically insecure young girl striving to enact the part of the *femme fatale* as Hollywood has outlined it for her: "Luck is just hard work, they say. . . ." "Acting is in my blood. We Greeners . . . were all theatre people. . . ." "I'd like to do a show on Broadway" (158). It is this very sense of the amateurishness of her performance that fascinates Tod: "Faye's affectations . . . were so completely artificial that he found them charming" (103).

In her aspiration to be a Hollywood sex siren Faye makes of herself a stereotype, "the grotesqueness of the screen made into real flesh," as James F. Light remarks (48). She is obliged to make of her body a marketable commodity, at the service of the Hollywood industry for films about dancing girls in Damascus, and of Audrey Jennings, whose brothel is in many ways a metaphor for the Hollywood "skin trade." The implied reduction of the woman to a marketable sex object in *The Day of the Locust* and *After Many a Summer* does not merely render the woman infertile, but dehumanizes her. Thus, her capacity for sympathy with others is reduced, as in the case of Virginia, or removed almost completely, as with Faye.

The combination of promiscuity with dehumanization is peculiar to the novels with a Hollywood or "natural museum" setting, suggesting, perhaps, that a woman in a rural/agricultural setting, even when she "goes astray," is still viewed as closer to a "natural" norm of womanly kindness, tenderness and protective nurturing. To call Armstrong's Belle Vasquez "a prostitute with a heart of gold" would be an overstatement; but she is a good-hearted prostitute, who retains a maternal sense of responsibility (albeit combined with much resentment) toward her deformed idiot son. She suggests at least a distant cousinship with de Maupassant's

Boule de Suif or Dostoevsky's Sonya. Yet her profession, viewed from the perspective of a patriarchal family ideal, makes a travesty of monogamic sexual relations. Even her motherhood is a parody of the single parenthood of the Virgin Mother to whom, like Huxley's Virginia Maunciple, she prays. Her child is not superhuman but subhuman; the child's father, instead of being benevolent and invisible is actively malevolent and all too clearly in evidence in the town which bears his name. Diseased and destitute, Belle ends her life by suicide. Unlike Hattie Rathbone, she never comes under the healing influence of Dave Washburn, or of his disciple, Hop Collins, who through the dissemination of their message of collective action will redeem society. She remains a parody of fulfilled motherhood to the end.

Hattie Rathbone, in her lonely childless state, parodies a patriarchal conception of woman as ideally fulfilled by nurturing and mothering. Her fulfillment, however, in the form of marriage to Hop Collins and potential motherhood, lacks the radical implications of Rose of Sharon's act of surrogate mothering in *The Grapes of Wrath* or even of the independent role played by Mabel Saugus in *Co-op*. Hattie's marriage returns her from independent if lonely self-sufficiency to a helpmeet role in relation to her husband-to-be, whose macho values she has brought herself to accept: "This was a hard world and men like Hop were its inheritors" (425). Hattie's choice is treated as correct and admirable. As Washburn's utopian program triumphs, woman, like the land, becomes fruitful. Hattie is enabled to approximate to the "earth-mother" norm, instead of being a parodic deviation from it.

In *The Grapes of Wrath* the three main female characters are all presented as potential earth-mothers. Ma Joad is the quintessential bearer, nurturer and comforter, wise in her patient endurance, capable of self-renewal. To her family she is "the citadel . . . the strong place that could not be taken" (79-80). Once pregnant, her daughter Rose of Sharon begins to take on the same appearance of wise maturity. With the changes in her body she acquires a "self-sufficient" smile, a "knowing-perfection look." The epithets suggest that in getting pregnant she has fulfilled her human destiny. Her once "hoydenish," provocative body is now "serious," but also "demure," seeming to imply that her past sexual activity and motherhood are antithetical, even incompatible terms. But Rose of Sharon's absorption in thoughts of pregnancy confers on her a dignity, a new exalted status. She is a "wise" creature, with something of a queenly air; her hair is arranged in a "crown". Her twelve-year-old sister Ruthie already shows the potential to be a nurturing mother-figure like the older women in the family, who feels the "responsibility of her developing breasts" (103).

When Rose of Sharon loses her child, she loses the dignity of motherhood. Just as California for the Joads has turned out to be a parody of Canaan, a place where the land's fruitfulness is wasted, so Rose of Sharon after her miscarriage becomes a parody of the earth-mother positively embodied by Ma Joad. She recovers, and indeed transcends, the original earth-mother ideal with her feeding of the starving migrant. As the Briffauldian model of matriarchal leadership evolves in the Joad family the nurturing of an actual baby becomes less important than the nurturing of a stranger, Ma Joad's "anybody," for whom she cares in an intuitive understanding of Casy's gospel of community. Her daughter Rose of Sharon becomes an example of a "new woman," combining within herself the admirable traits of the old ideal of the earth mother, but capable of a new breadth and depth of human sympathy transcending the limits of family obligation and of accepted convention.

One of Sinclair's female characters moves beyond the conventional wife/mother stereotype. Mabel Saugus is the co-author of a plan for the social salvation of California, one which she and her husband have "conceived" between them. She succeeds in being married, fertile, and to some extent "liberated" also—an achievement in keeping with the success of *Co-op*'s prophet-figures, and of its utopia. As an example of the socialist ideal of a "New Woman," Mabel Saugus, while she rejects neither monogamy nor heterosexual relationships, is idealized as capable, creative and intelligent in ways which take her outside the bounds of the domestic sphere.

The success of the prophet-figure's utopian program, and the woman's corresponding recovery of fertility, occur, as suggested in Chapter Two, only in an agrarian setting. The world of the "natural museum" of Hollywood and Los Angeles as presented in *After Many a Summer* and *The Day of the Locust* is inimical both to the preaching of utopia and to the fertility of women, who are parodies of the wife-and-mother ideal of womanhood. To what extent the settings of this world—the Stoyte castle, the Hollywood film set—themselves depend upon parody of a different ideal, is a question yet to be dealt with.

Notes

1 James Light, who views both Faye and Adore as "grotesques," draws a further analogy between the two characters: "The cheat of the purse that Adore offers is comparable to the lust which Faye offers instead of love. Both his deception and that of Faye are symbols of the larger lies purveyed by Hollywood" (49).

2 The one united family group in *The Day of the Locust* is that of the Gingos, who are, culturally speaking, peripheral to the California scene and also peripheral to the novel's development. The sole example in the novel of disinterested assistance of one human being by another, Mary Dove's consolation of Faye on the death of Faye's father, is undercut by the fact that Mary Dove solves Faye's financial difficulties by persuading her to become a prostitute.

3 The older writer was one of those to whom West sent proofs of *The Day of the Locust*. See Martin 323.

4 Robert E. Baker's comment that in *After Many a Summer* women characters "are rigidly confined to the three roles of saint, prostitute or a prurient conflation of both" (218) is largely accurate, except that the only "saints"—presumably Baker alludes to Jo Stoyte's Puritan grandmother and Christian Scientist wife—are both long since dead. It is Virginia, and Virginia's sexual preoccupations, that represent the novel's central female consciousness.

5 According to Baker, Huxley, as a crucial part of his strategy for advocating a "timeless" philosophy in *After Many a Summer*, attacks "the very ground of human experience of time—organic growth and sexual generation." In launching this attack, however, the novel also implies that some manifestations of sexuality—promiscuity, for example—are more undesirable and destructive than others (194). All enslavement to desire, though, entails enslavement to the world of time and appearance—to the *saeculum*.

6 She is Stoyte's baby, just as he is also "a little bit her baby and her patient" (45). The Stoyte castle itself represents, among other things, a womb in which the castle's inhabitants burrow away from self-knowledge and from social awareness. In this world, according to Peter Firchow, Virginia is, as her surname suggests, "official caterer" to the others' emotional and sexual needs.

7 Malin regards Faye's "gobbling" as an aspect of her predatory nature: "Her gobbling is symbolically justified—she devours all men in the novel to gain some perverse kind of nourishment" (96).

8 Tod at one point characterizes her as "a whore" (162).

9 In "Bird and Bottle," a short story published in 1936, Faye appears as a more sympathetic character than in *The Day of the Locust*. The story narrates the incident—the fight in the desert between Earle Shoop and Miguel—which later became Chapter Fourteen of the novel, but in the story events are described largely from Faye's perspective. Faye is "frightened" by the antagonism she has aroused between the two men, but her fear makes her "still more reckless." In the moment of her escape from the fight she feels "comfortably relaxed, even happy" (137). In *The Day of the Locust* these possibilities of sympathizing with, or at least having knowledge of, Faye's reactions to events, are removed. Viewed from the exterior, with detachment, Faye is made to seem repellingly alien.

10 In Steinbeck's *In Dubious Battle* an actual childbirth functions as an image of proletarian insurrection—and also as an occasion of communality among the migrant workers who, under the direction of two Communist labor organizers, (midwives of the revolution) assist with the birth. The irony of the fictional situation is that Mac and Jim present themselves to the masses as trained experts, when in fact they have no more idea what should be done to assist a birth than anyone else. History, Steinbeck's little parable seems to suggest, requires a minimum of obstetrical interference.

11 The conclusion of *Parched Earth* must leave the reader with a certain amount of confusion concerning Hattie's pregnancy. The father of the child is obviously not Tod Strawn, and the obvious candidate would seem to be Hop Collins. Yet on the morning of the day of the flood Hattie is shown regretting the thought that "there would be no Dickey" (the name she had chosen for the baby she hoped to have with Tod Strawn). As she climbs the windmill with the others, however, Hattie carries a box of baby clothes, "warm with the breath of a gurgling Dickey" (429). That Hattie will, if she has not already done so, bear a child, is evidently implied; and with this the reader has to be content.

12 Voluminous criticism has been written on the closing scene of *The Grapes of Wrath*, in which Rose of Sharon breast-feeds the starving stranger. For Clifton Fadiman, in a contemporary review of the film of *The Grapes of Wrath*, the scene in the novel was "the tawdriest kind of fake symbolism" (French 185). Celeste Turner Wright in 1955 traced analogues for the suckling of an adult in world literature and concluded that in Europe, at least until the mid-seventeenth century, "few decorous readers would have been startled by Rose of Sharon's method of preserving a life" (51). Howard Levant, in a 1974 study, expresses skepticism about the presentation of the change in Rose of Sharon's character which would make her mature and generous action possible (59). As I hope to have shown, the change develops more steadily, and more credibly, than Levant concedes. Moreover, Rose of

Sharon's act fits into a broader pattern of contemporary California fiction, in which a woman's capacity to give birth or to nurture is an important measure of a prophet-figure's success in finding acceptance of his utopian program.

13 Steinbeck firmly resisted suggestions by the editors at Viking that the scene should be prepared for by, for example, having Rose of Sharon previously acquainted with the starving man. "To make the man known to the Joads," he wrote in reply to these suggestions, "would warp the whole meaning" of the scene. Rose of Sharon's action of giving had, in Steinbeck's view, to involve emotional detachment from the recipient. The breast-giving should entail "no more sentiment than the giving of a piece of bread" (178).

14 For a discussion of the term "phalanx," and of its significance in Steinbeck's fiction, see Chapter Two.

15 In speculating on the origins of organized society, Briffault writes, "The social instinct . . . is a group development. All familial feeling . . . the essential foundation . . . of a social organization, is the direct product of prolonged maternal care, and does not exist apart from it" (57). This quotation is from the 1931 edition of *The Mothers*, that referred to by Steinbeck.

16 As Warren Motley points out in his article "From Patriarchy to Matriarchy: Ma Joad's Role in *The Grapes of Wrath*," to Briffault "matriarchy" connotes a set of social relationships "based on cooperation rather than power" (399). In Motley's words, "Steinbeck uses Ma Joad's heightened stature to suggest that the communal values Briffault associates with matriarchy might provide an alternative basis for authority in American society as a whole" (405).

17 The promise of the utopia of community is also suggested by the development in the novel of Ma Joad's younger children, Ruthie and Winfield. Not only do they represent the future, but their childish squabbles offer a further example of predatory individualism. It is the children's quarrel over a box of popcorn that leads to the betrayal of Tom Joad and his forced parting from the family. Yet Ruthie is also shown overcoming her predatory tendencies, her impulse to domineer over others. In the slight but significant scene which immediately precedes Rose of Sharon's suckling of the stranger, Ruthie is shown making a conscious choice to share with her small brother (499).

18 For example, Rose of Sharon blames Tom for having avenged the murder of Casy: "An' now you kill a fella. What chance that baby got to get bore right?" (435).

19 "Tom's chances of staying alive, much less of relieving his people's oppression, are slim. The uncertainty of his future reflects Steinbeck's pessimism not only about the labor movement's prospects, but also about curbing the anti-social effects of individualism" (412).

However, Motley qualifies this skepticism by remarking on the imaginative power of the scene of Tom's parting from his mother and on the "symbolic" importance of Tom's decision to follow Casy.

20 See for example the story "Breakfast," part of which Steinbeck incorporated into Chapter Twenty-Two of *The Grapes of Wrath*, in which the nursing of the baby at the breast forms an essential background to the simple, undramatic set of experiences which yet contain for the narrator "some element of great beauty" (Covici 420).

21 Much recent discussion of Steinbeck's work has centered on the question of his attitudes to women. Fontenrose has noted Steinbeck's idealization of sexless mother-figures (129). Falkenberg, in a 1975 study of "Female Characterization in Steinbeck's Fiction," remarks on the reduction of female roles in Steinbeck's work to those of wife and mother (51). Marilyn Mitchell discusses Steinbeck's success in humanizing and individualizing the "earth-mother" stereotype (91). Interestingly, the stereotyping of Huxley's Virginia Maunciple or of West's Faye Greener, despite the quantities of criticism on Huxley and West, seems to have gone largely unremarked.

22 If one takes seriously Spivak's suggestion that the traditional marxian account of the relations between labor and production needs emendation to include consideration of the womb as a place of material production, then to speak of the "fruit" or produce of a woman's womb is more than a metaphor. (See *In Other Worlds* 79-80.)

Chapter Four

Museum/Mausoleum

After Many a Summer and *The Day of the Locust* portray Southern California as a museum, and a mausoleum. These museum/mausoleum images—along with pervasive motifs of imitation and contrived illusion—contrast sharply with the rural/agricultural settings of *After Many a Summer*, *The Grapes of Wrath*, *Parched Earth* and *Co-op*; contexts for the development of various utopias of community, and for the "cure" of barrenness in women. Just as the rural/agricultural setting is one in which community and mutuality develop, and in which life and organic growth are engendered, so in the "natural museum" of Southern California, isolation, artificiality, stasis and death are the norms.

For Randall Reid, in his 1967 study of Nathanael West, *No Redeemer, No Promised Land*, the image of Southern California presented in West's *The Day of the Locust* is that of a "natural museum." Hollywood is depicted as both a "dream factory" and a "dream dump."[1] It is both the "source" and the depository of the dreams by which Americans live. Southern California, or "Hollywood-Southland" as Walter Wells refers to it, is, moreover, the scene of violence and destructive sexuality in both *The Day of the Locust* and *After Many a Summer*.[2] Yet Los Angeles, the "City of the Angels," capital city of West's "land of sunshine and oranges," is also an element in the California Dream, a central feature of the geography of the Promised Land. As with the Canaan of California's agrarian setting, the inevitable consequence of such idealization of Hollywood-Southland is disillusionment. As Warwick Wadlington comments on *The Day of the Locust*, "West's Second Jerusalem has already been bought, built, and sold out . . ." (317).[3] The architecture and society of Southern California as depicted in *After Many a Summer* and *The Day of the Locust* represent yet one more parody of the Promised Land—one, however, which insofar as it is an "artificial," as opposed to a "natural" or agrarian setting, is portrayed as not susceptible to the transforming power of a prophet's utopia.[4]

As already noted, *After Many a Summer* and *The Day of the Locust* present Southern California as a site for the deposit of the accumulated detritus of Western "civilization." This characterization is not unconnected with the compulsive pursuit of wealth which takes place in both novels. One is reminded, for example, of Norman O. Brown's discussion of the compulsive accumulation of property as motivated by an infantile wish to deny the knowledge of death.[5] According to Brown, to be possessed as property objects have to be viewed as "crystallized time"—in psychoanalytic terms, as excrement. The modern city is itself crystallized time/excrement —an agglomerate produced by the collective activity of numerous accumulators of property—and always, despite repression of the knowledge of death, potentially a necropolis.[6] Reid's "natural museum" of Southern California, therefore, is also a "natural mausoleum." Especially in *After Many a Summer*, but also in *The Day of the Locust*, the images of museum and mausoleum overlap constantly.[7]

The Beverly Pantheon, Huxley's satirically depicted version of Forest Lawn in *After Many a Summer*, is both necropolis and museum. Like Forest Lawn, its chief feature, and the source of its chief appeal to the public, is its capacity to deal with death by denying it. In an eerie transposition, which the Pantheon's managers in *After Many a Summer* call "injecting sex appeal into death," Thanatos is made to assume the mask of Eros through the use of naked female statuary to decorate the cemetery's grounds, thus proclaiming the apparent "victory no longer of the spirit but of the body, the well-fed body, for ever youthful, immortally athletic, indefatigably sexy" (14). The converse of the Pantheon's "injection" of "sex-appeal" into death is the deliberate avoidance of "any representation of . . . any symbol of mortality." The policy is a resounding success: "Anyone who complained that there was no Crucifixion in the place could be referred to the published accounts" (202).

Although a graveyard, the Beverly Pantheon is also, like the castle home of its founder Jo Stoyte, a kind of museum. It contains a replica of the church of the Holy Trinity at Stratford-on-Avon, "complete with Shakespeare's tomb" (14). There are imitation catacombs, "miniature monuments of bogus antiquity," which are to be painted with fake murals (204). If the Pantheon's antiquities are bogus, their lack of authenticity, along with the cremation urns that resemble athletic trophies and the ubiquitous statuary, does not detract from the overall impression of the Beverly Pantheon as a museum, the accumulation of whose artifacts is designed to repress the knowledge of death.

The other conspicuous monument of *After Many a Summer*, Jo Stoyte's castle-museum, is of course drawn from San Simeon, William Randolph Hearst's castle retreat. As Frank Baldanza has pointed out, in *After Many a Summer* the Hearst castle's original site is moved two hundred miles south to the San Fernando Valley, "just outside Los Angeles" (446)[8]. This change of location not only places Huxley's fictional castle in the heart of Hollywood-Southland, but makes it possible for the Beverly Pantheon on the outskirts of Los Angeles to be all the more closely associated with Forest Lawn. Furthermore, the closeness of the fictional castle to the fictional cemetery invites comparison between them in the novel. If the Beverly Pantheon gives the appearance of a museum, the Stoyte castle with its heterogeneous collection of statuary, paintings, "lingams and stage-coaches," its cellars crammed with totem-poles and stuffed orangutans, its rooms representing the history of interior decoration from seventeenth-century India to early nineteenth-century Europe, is museum from foundations to ceiling. With its mummified nuns buried in a Roman sarcophagus under a Jacobean funerary sculpture, it is to some degree an extension of the Beverly Pantheon, just as the Pantheon represents an extension of the miscellaneous collection of antiquities in the Stoyte castle-museum. Metaphorically speaking, the castle is the tomb of Stoyte's ego, a tomb that his compulsion for acquisition and a desire to displace the social and personal have rendered attractive to him in his striving to escape the knowledge of death. Like the Pantheon, the castle is the site of a frantic quest to deny the present and the death that looms over it.[9] Stoyte, like his historical counterpart William Randolph Hearst, is neurotically frightened of the idea of death; an employee who imprudently points out to Stoyte his future grave-site in the Beverly Pantheon is immediately dismissed. The Stoyte castle becomes the site of experiments designed to find a method of prolonging Stoyte's life indefinitely.

The Hollywood back lot in *The Day of the Locust* where Tod wanders in search of Faye has, like the Beverly Pantheon and the Stoyte castle in *After Many a Summer*, characteristics of both a museum and a mausoleum. The appropriate artists to represent it, Tod considers, would be Rosa, Guardi and Desiderio, "the painters of Decay and Mystery." The studio lot is a "Sargasso of the imagination," a "history of civilization" in the form of a "dream dump" that represents that history through its miscellaneous debris (132). The wooden horse of Troy here shares a last resting place with the skeleton of a Zeppelin, a Mayan temple, "part of the Fourteenth Street elevated station," and the bones of a dinosaur (131). The dream dump is not a static quantity; its contents constantly expand: "The dump grew continually, for there wasn't a dream afloat somewhere which wouldn't sooner or later turn up on it, having first been made photographic by plaster, canvas, lath and paint" (132). The Hollywood back lot is, in Norman O. Brown's phrase, "a deposit of accumulated sublimation"—a monument to death which at the same time denies death through the accumulation of objects, "crystallized" time.[10] Among the jumble of façades of buildings representing different historical periods is a Greek temple dedicated to Eros. Appropriately enough in this realm of Thanatos which is the Hollywood back lot the god Eros, his sovereignty overthrown, lies "face downward in a pile of old newspapers" (131). West's Hollywood, like Huxley's Beverly Pantheon, represents that last stage of the polis which is "Nekropolis."

"'I don't care how much cellophane she wraps it in,' he said—'nautch joints are depressing, like all places for deposit, banks, mail boxes, tombs . . . '" (72). This remark of Tod Hackett's, as he allows a fellow-sexist-screen artist to persuade him to visit a local brothel, alludes to a pervasive metaphor in *The Day of the Locust*. To Tod's list of "depressing" places for deposit a variety of museums can be added: the cabinet of miniature dogs at Audrey Jennings' brothel, and the Hollywood suburbs representing a variety of anachronistic architectural styles (an example of the museum which, with its emphasis on imitation and contrived illusion, will require fuller consideration later in this chapter). There is also the funeral home where the dead Harry Greener is put on display, one room of which, (with its model tombstones and its "framed photographs of important funerals" on the walls) is yet another version of the museum (126). The overall effect of this emphasis on the museum—which, as in the description of the funeral home, is sometimes also a mausoleum—is to remind the reader of the burden of the past, of the passage of time, and of the "dead end" which the accumulation of objects inevitably proves to be for the individual in flight from death.

In both *After Many a Summer* and *The Day of the Locust*, the living are themselves presented as leading a deathlike existence. The characters in Jo Stoyte's castle are rigorously fixed personalities, in Huxleyan terms, "entombed" in their egos. Jeremy Pordage is obsessed with literary scholarship to the exclusion of everything else, and lives under the domination of his possessive mother, even in her absence. Obispo derives pleasure from sadistic destructiveness, from manipulating and dominating both Virginia Maunciple and his employer, Stoyte. Virginia herself lives a largely "mindless" existence, in which only the pleasures of the moment have any meaning for her. Jo Stoyte, in his terror of aging, will in the end accept the prospect of a subhuman existence as an ape as preferable to death. His obsession with death, paradoxically, reduces his capacity fully to experience life, since his days are spent in dread of his end. At the same time Stoyte blights the lives of others through his bullying, his meanness, his obsession with wielding power and his contempt for others. As William Propter points out, when the life of the man from Kansas who picks fruit on Jo Stoyte's estate is reduced and narrowed by poverty, Stoyte and the social values he upholds are largely to blame.

Images of a death which gives the illusion of life are pervasive in *After Many a Summer*, from the tomb statuary of the Beverly Pantheon to the promises of resurrection made by the preacher at Pete Boone's funeral and heard by William Propter with skepticism, to the image of the ape mother compulsively grooming her dead baby. These images, when linked to the deathlike existences of the characters, create an atmosphere of death surrounding them and serve as context, metaphorically produced, for evoking a sense of the malaise of a society whose real values are manifested through greed and predatory behavior.[11]

Although the diagnosis of society's malaise is less clearly formulated than in *After Many a Summer*, images of death in the midst of life, or of death which mimics life, are prevalent in *The Day of the Locust*. As in *After Many a Summer*, characters exist in deathlike states. Homer Simpson, after his desertion by Faye, attempts "uterine flight." He seeks a return to a nurturing matrix which Tod Hackett appears to envy: "What a warm, rich darkness. The grave wasn't in it" (171). In fact, in the course of his passive, solitary existence, Homer has merely inhabited a series of such apparent refuges: hotel rooms, an isolated house. In his reduced existence he appears to be "sleep-walking or partially blind" (88). Only encounters with women arouse him; and then only to an experience of pain, and, finally, only one of violence, as he attacks a little boy. The anonymous mid-Westerners who have settled in California react against the crushing boredom of their existence in a similar way, by participating in the Hollywood riot. While these characters exist in a state of deathlike passivity, at least one character, Harry Greener, is physically sick and dying. While the passivity of Homer mimics death, the corpse of Harry lying in Holsepp's funeral parlor, with its shaven face and artificially ruddy cheeks, is an example of death giving the illusion of life. Greener is referred to as "Harry" and "he" as if the dead man were indeed merely sleeping, "snug" in his box (125).

Images in *The Day of the Locust* often seem to indicate a vitality which, on closer inspection, proves to be a reminder of death or of sterility. In the description of the undergrowth surrounding the studio back lot, for instance, the narrator's choice of language lends to nature a suffering and an aggressive aspect, suggesting that here organic life struggles for mere existence. The debris of the back lot is surrounded by "tortured" trees, whose "exposed roots writhed dramatically in the arid ground," and by thorns described as "armories of spikes, hooks and swords" (132). Similarly, Homer Simpson's "garden," which, like the Beverly Pantheon in *After Many a Summer* is at least nominally a little oasis overlooking a desert canyon turns out to be a barren enclosure occupied by rusty cans and "the remains" of a group of "ragged, tortured," scarcely surviving cactus plants. The garden's only other living things are a lizard and the flies the lizard preys upon. Aggression and destruction are again stressed in the scenes in the desert which end with a fight between Earle Shoop and Miguel over Faye.[12] Amid the gaudy colors of the desert rocks appear the "glittering particles" of a hummingbird in flight, chasing a marauding jay like a "ruby bullet" (113). The aggressiveness of the birds and the bright colors of their plumage invite association with the colorful feathers of Miguel's murderous fighting-cocks—images of violent, destructive sexuality (114). The scenes in the desert conclude, in fact, with the drawing of explicit analogies between human and animal behavior; with Tod, "hound-like," tracking Faye, who elsewhere in the novel is likened to a hunted game bird and to a deer and who, like Tod, is one of West's life-emptied characters (117, 174). On the film set of *Waterloo* dead men appear to come to life. *The Day of the Locust* opens with the passing of a ghost army over the scene: "It moved like a mob; its lines broken, as though fleeing from some terrible defeat. The dolmans of the hussars, the heavy shakos of the guards ... jumbled together in bobbing disorder" (59). The appearance of this routed ghost army and the sense of disorientation it produces are described for half a page before the illusion is broken by the arrival of a director wielding a megaphone, and the reader is allowed to know that this is a description of a film set. Like the flags of bright flame that in Tod's vision of the burning of Los Angeles give even the anticipated "terrible holocaust" a "gala air," the appearance of these ghosts upon the Hollywood film set gives the setting a hades-like quality.[13]

Destructive energy, life devoted to death, is evident in the human acts of violence which occur in both *After Many a Summer* and *The Day of the Locust*. In *After Many a Summer*, there are Stoyte's constant outbursts of paranoid rage, which finally lead to his jealous killing of Pete Boone. In *The Day of the Locust*, besides the violence of the riot at the film première, there is the series of fights between Faye's lovers.[14] There is also Faye's destructive cruelty to Homer, which by disturbing him emotionally helps motivate the riot. This riot demonstrates, above all, the pent-up frustrations which make virtually every character in the novel a potential destroyer. In its occurrence under the guise of a festive occasion—and in the disturbing cheerfulness of some of the crowd's members as they fantasize about acts of violence—the motif of destructive vitality is developed in the novel's climax.

A further, not unrelated, feature of both novels is their emphasis on various types of fake imitation and contrived illusion. These, in turn, seem to be related to a shared feature of the human imagination as a perverse and desperate inventive power that reshapes the material environment in a wish-fulfillment of desires repressed, deferred or frustrated in actuality.

After Many a Summer and *The Day of the Locust* both present satirically the activities of characters who piece together protective shells out of whatever fragments come to hand to "shore against their ruins"—to shield their sterility and emptiness. These protective shells may be regarded, in fact, as extensions of the museum. Jo Stoyte's castle full of art objects and Faye Greener's "pack" of film scenarios are only two examples of the novels' archives of dreams—archives which, like the Beverly Pantheon, are designed to ward off the knowledge of death.

The architecture of Los Angeles is portrayed in both novels as having more than a passing affinity with that of the film set, in its colorfulness, flimsiness, and above all its purpose of realizing the owners' dreams of flight from quotidian actuality. Jeremy Pordage in *After Many a Summer* sees from the car, on his way to the Stoyte castle, a succession of synagogues in the style of Hagia Sophia, Christian Science churches that resemble banks, and a restaurant in the shape of a bulldog (5). Like Tod Hackett, in his encounter with the fake architecture of the film set previously referred to, Pordage sees the "façades" of houses (the word suggests film sets rather than solid three-dimensional buildings) which are almost all imitative of architectural styles: "pastiches" of Lutyens manor houses; "light-hearted parodies" of Le Corbusier; "fantastic . . . adaptations" of Mexican haciendas. To Pordage they resemble nothing so much as "the pavilions at some endless international exhibition" (10-11). In *The Day of the Locust* too, architecture has a strong affinity with the film set, being fantastic, colorful, flimsily constructed, and above all intended to suggest escape from a suffocating boredom and anxiety.[15] Like the buildings in *After Many a Summer*, houses in *The Day of the Locust* represent a range of fantastic styles, from miniature Rhine castles to a "shack" with oriental domes and minarets. "It is hard to laugh at the need for beauty and romance," Tod reflects as he contemplates these architectural disasters, but "Few things are sadder than the truly monstrous" (61). The artificiality extends to a house interior in which machine-made hinges are stamped to appear forged by hand and furniture is painted to look unpainted (81).

Other "dream archives" are apparent in the clothing and mannerisms of characters in *After Many a Summer* and *The Day of the Locust*. In *After Many a Summer*, Jeremy Pordage is surprised by the sight of a woman shopping downtown in a fur jacket and a swimsuit (10). Virginia Maunciple wears a yachting cap to ride her scooter. In *The Day of the Locust* the everyday clothing of the Los Angeles citizens is explicitly described as resembling "fancy dress" (60).

Characters exhibit affected behavior and/or identify strongly with their social roles. Jo Stoyte loves to parade his lack of education, to emphasize his character of "self-made" man (25). The chauffeur who works for Jo Stoyte does a disconcerting impersonation of a family retainer in the Old South (4). Virginia Maunciple's gestures resemble those of a woman taking a screen test, who is required to register emotions on demand (88). Affected behavior and role-playing are pervasive in *The Day of the Locust*, too. Tod's fellow-screenwriter, Claude Estee, pretends to be a Southern Civil War colonel and affects a paunch he does not possess (68). Faye Greener's father Harry acts the part of a sick man, even when he actually is gravely ill. Abe Kusich assumes an aggressive manner toward his friends which is "often a joke" (66). Faye Greener's affections are "so completely artificial" as to be "charming" to Tod Hackett (103).

The obsession with accumulation of objects and the imitations and impersonations which characters in *After Many a Summer* and *The Day of the Locust* practice are, above all, a symptom of the obsessive, hopeless desire to escape subjection to time. Stoyte's castle represents flight from the past—his conspicuous display of wealth is in part an attempt to repudiate an impoverished childhood, of which the sight of the migrant workers on his estate all too painfully reminds him (124). More important, though, is the castle's function of shutting out thought of the future—especially of Stoyte's imminent death. Stoyte's obsession with the accumulation of possessions in his castle-museum serves a purpose not very different from that served by the statues in the Beverly Pantheon—of denying the inevitable effects of time and decay. His mistress

Virginia succeeds better than Stoyte in excluding both the past and the present from her consciousness, dwelling in a "mindless eternity" of pleasures; at least until Obispo awakens her sense of guilt. Jeremy Pordage manages to escape from the present moment, into a world of words, and preoccupation with another version of the "museum," the library. Only William Propter is presented as having an appropriate attitude to the world of time—a point which will be considered later in further detail. It is Stoyte's obsession with time and aging, however, which dominates the greater part of *After Many a Summer*. Despite his elaborate efforts to escape the idea—and even the fact—of aging, Stoyte is reminded by the Beverly Pantheon of his own death and burial (205). He is presented, not without sympathy, as an "old, unhappy, frightened man" (212).

The characters in *The Day of the Locust* are also obsessed in various ways with time: Harry Greener with his past glory as a comedian, Faye his daughter with fantasies of some indefinite future when she will be a star. Most important for an understanding of the characters' investment in fantasy, however—and hence of their share in creating the Hollywood "dream dump"—is the projection of dreams and hopes by the mid-Westerners who come to California, into a future which always slides away before them like a mirage. The arid emptiness of their present existence is a torment to them. These dreamers of the California Dream "have been cheated and betrayed."[16] The vision of a future of "sunshine and oranges" for which the retired mid-Westerners have "saved and slaved" all their lives, in the actuality of the present turns out to be hollow (178). The middle-aged and the old, with only the end of their lives before them, are the most "savage and bitter" (177). The sense that their future holds only emptiness, that they will never enjoy the fullness of life, causes them to "burn with resentment" (178).

The frustration of the mid-Westerners perpetuates their compulsive dreaming and dream-chasing. They follow funerals and film-stars; they go to the airport in the hope of seeing a plane crash. They join the cults which teach "brain-breathing of the Aztecs," or that of Dr. Know-All Pierce-All with his raw food diet fad. But they also crave "stimulation through violence," and will sympathize vicariously with Tod's torch-bearers, in the burning of

Los Angeles. Some of those who "come to California to die"[17] will actually take part in the destruction, following in "a great united front of screwballs and screwboxes to purify the land" (184). Their hysteria is infectious; the normally inoffensive Homer both shares the hysteria and becomes its victim; and so does Tod Hackett, who in rescuing a woman from being molested during the riot at the film première with which *The Day of the Locust* ends, seizes hold of a man's ear and finds himself hoping the ear "would come away in his hand" (182).

The museum-mausoleums of both *The Day of the Locust* and *After Many a Summer* are presented as ineffectual defenses against a dread of the passage of time and a sense of the inadequacy of everyday existence which various versions of the California Dream—retirement in the sun, a castle with orange groves, religious cults, the hope of stardom—fail to dispel. The predator-victims, Stoyte, Faye, Tod, are, like others, dupes of the dream of the good life that has brought each to California. Whether Southern California fulfills the migrant's dream of the Promised Land, or whether, as for the most part, it merely parodies it, the result is a disillusionment which leads to a frantic quest for means of escape—to construction of the dream-palace, the museum, the mausoleum. The images of the museum/mausoleum and the related motif of imitation, then, are representative of the collective flight from the underlying knowledge of the futility of these dreams. When the frustration engendered by this repressed knowledge erupts, the result is violence and destruction.

After Many a Summer has been called Huxley's "Hollywood" novel[18]—an accurate description only if it refers to the novel's setting of Southern California with its references to Los Angeles. The only characters connected with Hollywood to appear in it, in fact, are Virginia Maunciple's starlet friends, who receive but a passing mention. In *The Day of the Locust*, on the other hand, the film world provides the central metaphor of the museum/mausoleum—the "dream dump" of the studio lot. Moreover, it functions, as the images of the Stoyte castle-museum and of the Beverly Pantheon in *After Many a Summer* cannot do, not only as the repository of dreams, but also as their instigator, as the chief source and fountain-head of all those fantasies which hold the human imagination in thrall. In the last analysis Hollywood motivates not only Faye Greener's delusions of grandeur, but the fantastic architecture of the Los Angeles streets near the studios—true parodies of a New Jerusalem, with streets of gold—and the obsession, at once pathetic and sinister, a compound of fascination and hatred—of the retired "fans" from the mid-West who follow the stars around.[19] Moreover, whereas Stoyte clings to material objects, for which, paradoxically, he feels contempt and hatred (except insofar as they demonstrate his wealth and economic security), the followers of the California Dream in *The Day of the Locust* cherish largely insubstantial hopes, dreams and ambitions which Hollywood represents for them.

As suggested earlier, the images of a museum as a mausoleum, in the Stoyte castle and the Hollywood dream dump, and of a mausoleum as a museum, in the Beverly Pantheon and the Holsepp funeral parlor, are central to both novels. These motifs are more subtly handled in *The Day of the Locust*, where images of "places for deposit" recur throughout. Above all, this conception of the interrelationship of studio lot, brothel, funeral parlor, and of the "bonfire of architectural styles" which makes of the entire architectural archive of Los Angeles one vast funeral pyre in Tod Hackett's imagination, emphasizes the collective death wish, which, given the failure of the California Dream and the absence in the novel of any utopian alternative, possesses the imagination of the characters in this novel.

In presenting human violence and destructiveness, Huxley's novel ranges in time and space, introducing allusions to the Spanish Civil War and to the eighteenth-century slave-trading activities of a fictional Earl of Gonister. *The Day of the Locust*, on the other hand, depicts only Hollywood, Los Angeles and its surroundings. This close connection between the immediate setting and its metaphoric overtones of museum/mausoleum—or, as in the scenes in the desert, of arid and savage terrain, a setting for violence—makes of West's social critique a very specific indictment of Southern Californian society, and of its California Dream.[20] *After Many a Summer*, notwithstanding its locally sponsored attacks on the predatory lifestyle of a Stoyte, its denunciation of the working and living conditions imposed on migrant agricultural workers, its satire (of bogus swamis, inane film scenarios, bizarre architecture, and the Californian way of death), also makes a general statement about the "universal" human condition; a condition which, in the narrator's view, only self-transcendence can cure. In West, violence, like that between Faye's jealous lovers, appears to arise directly out of the tensely charged atmosphere of the Hollywood setting, which will incubate the full-fledged riot of the film première. In Huxley, violence, while it clearly has local causes—the jealous possessiveness of a Stoyte, for example—is not peculiarly a feature of the California scene. It is treated as part of the price paid by unenlightened human nature for remaining in a state of unenlightenment.

It has already been noted that both *After Many a Summer* and *The Day of the Locust* treat various forms of imitation and contrived illusion as characteristic of the wish-fulfillment, and the flight from the knowledge of death, of those individuals who pursue various versions of the California Dream, and that these imitations, whether in architecture, clothing or mannerisms, are themselves an extension of the image of the museum. The two novels make use of another, related, form of imitation—pastiche of different verbal styles, and of literary allusions.[21] In *After Many a Summer* such imitation is restricted to a humorous pastiche of *True Confessions* (27), of the billboards of Los Angeles (5-6), of a piece of academic oratory (291-93), and of the eighteenth-century diary of the Earl of Gonister. In *The Day of the Locust*, characters themselves at least partly consciously mimic verbal styles in order to give substance and a spurious credibility to their assumed characters. Not surprisingly, their models are often derived from the film world. Faye Greener uses the clichés she has learned from the trade papers and fan magazines (158). Abe Kusich speaks the language of the Hollywood detective film: "So you're a wise guy, hah, a know-it-all . . ." "That's what I get for fooling with four-bit broads . . ." "I'll get you fixed up swell" (64-66). Claude Estee employs the screen dialogue of a Southern Civil War colonel: "Here, you black rascal! A mint julep" (69). Characters' use of screen-derived dialogue in this way is not only a further indication of the centrality and importance of Hollywood in West's fictional world in *The Day of the Locust*—but represents a further extension of the museum motif, in that their very speech is an archive of these various verbal styles.

In *After Many a Summer*, Jo Stoyte is clearly identified as the character in the novel most responsible not only for the sufferings of himself and others, but for the sustaining of the California Dream. In the admiration his wealth and power evoke in those around him, his status is shown to exercise an ideological and economic influence over others' lives. It is Stoyte's neurotic habit of wealth accumulation and his dread of dying, furthermore, which motivate the building of the Stoyte castle and the Beverly Pantheon, visible manifestations of the Natural Museum.

In *The Day of the Locust*, on the other hand, the builders of the Natural Museum and promoters of the Dream are largely invisible. The novel contains very few references to the entrepreneurs who control the finances and determine the content of the Hollywood dream palace. Apart from passing references to "a Charles H. Grotenstein Production," and to Kahn's Persian Palace Theatre, where the film première is held, the names of these guardians and promoters are left unrevealed. The effect of this presentation of the Hollywood scene, with its focus on very average people, the middle-class followers of the California Dream, is to create a world of the "Cheated" (as West himself referred to them) who, not knowing whom to blame for their disillusionment, vent their destructive rage upon one another.[22]

This difference in presentation of the promoters and victims of the Dream and of the builders of the Natural Museum, is not without its effect on the portrayal of social relations. In *After Many a Summer* these relations are hierarchical, and focus almost entirely on individuals whose economic welfare depends directly or indirectly on Jo Stoyte. At the apex of the social pyramid is Stoyte, whose economic influence extends to the boards of insurance and oil companies, to agricultural estates and banks. At its base are the migrant workers whom he exploits. In its intermediate ranks are the less prosperous capitalists who depend on Stoyte's goodwill and on the fluctuations of the market, the professional employees like Obispo and Pordage, the estate managers, nurses, cooks and chauffeurs. By concentrating on Stoyte's domestic arrangements on his estate, the narrator succeeds in demonstrating how many of the social relationships of capitalist California in the 1930s resemble feudal ones, except that the law sets stricter limits to Stoyte's power over his employees. Correspondingly, Stoyte's version of the museum/mausoleum is one in which—even though the contents of the museum are disorientingly jumbled—each individual has a clearly defined economic, social and physically-defined "place": Obispo in his laboratory, Pordage in the library, Virginia in her boudoir, the migrant workers in their hovels outside the castle walls.

The Day of the Locust presents not a many-leveled social hierarchy, but rather two loosely interrelated groups that interact socially and are distinguished from one another not by employer-employee relations but by the degree of their economic security. One consists of individuals (they can scarcely be regarded as constituting a class) of slender, often precarious means—squatters, out-of-work cowboys and film extras, and racing touts; and the other of members of the "respectable" middle class, people in professional employment, like Tod Hackett and Claude Estee, or retired, like Homer Simpson and the other mid-Westerners who "come to California to die" (60). West's narrator, furthermore, emphasizes the rootless character of these middle-class "Cheated" in the description of the crowd who riot at the film première, largely composed of "the lower middle classes." These have financial, but not emotional, security. "Every other person" in the crowd is one of Hackett's "torchbearers" (177). They riot, it is true, in the name of values they share with the film producers and other manufacturers of the Hollywood version of the California Dream; but the emotionally frustrated middle classes are treated by the narrator as the natural adherents of, and the natural breeding ground for, a mass movement of destructive fanatics. Hackett sees them as capable of initiating nationwide civil war: "The Angelenos would be first, but their comrades all over the country would follow" (118).[23] The desperation of these people is compounded by their lack of definite social identity. They are retired, and hence without job status, and live in rented homes furnished by others. If the version of the Natural Museum in *After Many a Summer* is a feudal castle in which each individual is assigned a definite place, that of *The Day of the Locust* is a film studio in which individuals constantly shift roles, and even the background scenery never ceases to change.

After Many a Summer and *The Day of the Locust* differ not only in their presentation of the context of social malaise, and identification of those responsible for it, but in the conception of the relation of the prophet-figure's vision to that context. The social and economic precepts of the prophet-figure of *After Many a Summer* are largely formulated in response to and as an alternative to the values of Jo Stoyte.[24] Propter's social utopia, while it rests on an assumption of the achievability of particular "spiritual" goals, is one in which "the fewest possible opportunities" would arise for the Jo Stoytes of the world "to realize their potentialities" (147).[25] In *The Day of the Locust* no such pair of clear-cut alternatives is presented. Significantly, Tod Hackett, unlike Propter with his rural dwelling on the outskirts of the Natural Museum setting, actually inhabits the Natural Museum and is even imbued with some of its values. This situation offers him no standpoint from which a viable utopian alternative to existing conditions might be developed.

Not only does *The Day of the Locust* lack any positive utopia,[26] but the reader cannot be certain to what extent even Tod Hackett's nihilistic vision of the burning of the museum/mausoleum of Los Angeles is communicated to others. The narrator of *The Day of the Locust* mentions a completed painting of "The Burning of Los Angeles" in which Tod's prophetic vision is expressed—a picture which, in the narrator's view, "definitely proved he had talent"—but the narrator seems able to recognize the models for each of the figures in the painting, Faye among them (108, 184-85). He refers to them by their first names in a way which suggests intimacy with Tod and his circle. There is no suggestion, then, that Tod has "proved" his talent to the world at large, or reached a broader public.

With his vision of a destructive mob composed not only of the voyeuristic mid-Westerners, and of religious cultists,[27] but of economic ones, Hackett closes off the last possibility of a rational social utopia (184). Mindless, purposeless violence is the only conceivable outcome of the frustration depicted in *The Day of the Locust*, given the absence of any such positive utopia capable of allaying it. The Natural Museum has failed to fulfill its purpose of allaying the fears and frustrations of the California Dreamers. The Torchbearers among them will burn it down.

The lack of any positive utopian vision in *The Day of the Locust* seems not unconnected with the absence in the novel of an agrarian setting. Neither Hollywood Boulevard, with its dropouts, touts, prostitutes and struggling film extras, nor the world of the movie set, nor Earle's and Miguel's world of desert squatters, seems conducive to the development of utopia. (Even in *After Many a Summer* a utopia can be developed only where conditions are literally as well as figuratively fertile—where there is an expanse of cultivable earth—but not within the confines of the Stoyte castle-museum). If California's artificial and urban settings of the Natural Museum parody the New Jerusalem, they, unlike the agrarian setting which is a parody of Eden and/or Canaan, remain untransformed and unredeemed.

As in *Parched Earth* and *The Grapes of Wrath*, the settings of *After Many a Summer* and *The Day of the Locust* are used to present implicit critiques of the California Dream, which the novels' prophet-figures make explicitly. In *After Many a Summer* and *The Day of the Locust* they not only present an urban world which is, as Wadlington has suggested, a parody of the Second Jerusalem (or the New Jerusalem), but the Southern California/ Los Angeles/Hollywood setting supplies a metaphor for the destructiveness that underlies the allure of the California Dream. The violence which erupts at the close of both novels—Stoyte's shooting of Pete Boone, the riot at the film première—is representative and expressive of frustrations repressed through investment in versions of the Dream. "Hollywood-Southland" in *After Many a Summer* and *The Day of the Locust*, by means of the Stoyte castle, the Beverly Pantheon, the studio back lot, and descriptions of local architecture, is presented as a museum which is also a mausoleum, as a version of the polis that is also, actually or potentially, Nekropolis. The possibility of the growth of some form of utopian alternative to the existing ideology and the existing social malaise in the two novels is presented as either restricted in scope (Propter's marginal community), or, as in *The Day of the Locust*, non-existent and substituted by a prophetic vision of mass destruction. Utopia, it seems, will flourish in California in a rural setting—in the community in the eucalyptus grove, in the growing sense of interdependence of migrants on the road, in the solidarity at a campsite of homeless workers who will inherit the earth; but not in the shadow of the Natural Museum. In the latter setting, utopia is wholly supplanted by a frantic attachment to existing ideology, or by a critique of that ideology which finds nothing with which to replace it. The Natural Museum turns out to be a Beverly Pantheon, in which the knowledge of death is concealed, yet constantly inadvertently revealed, exposing the fundamentally destructive nature of this version of the California Dream.

Notes

1 Reid argues that West uses the museum image "to explore the natural world of Southern California, a world which lures representative victims of every dream." Hollywood is for West, according to Reid, "both a dream factory and a dream dump, the source and termination of all those manufactured visions which flicker through the lives of people who, at last, come to California, but only to die" (115).

2 See *Tycoons and Locusts* 123. Wells finds that throughout *The Day of the Locust*, "sexuality is alternately confused, debased, and destroyed" (52).

3 Walter Allen found in *The Day of the Locust* a "sour comment" upon *The Grapes of Wrath* and on the "almost instinctive westward drive it celebrates" (170). Further support for Allen's speculation may perhaps be found in the fact that West considered sending a copy of *The Day of the Locust* to Steinbeck for his evaluation (Martin 323). *The Grapes of Wrath*, however, in its disillusioned presentation of California as a parody of Eden and/or Canaan, hardly "celebrates" westward migration as uncritically as Allen suggests.

4 Wadlington's architectural metaphor seems most apposite in its stress on the artificial construction of the Hollywood setting. In his comment on Los Angeles/Hollywood as "the Second Jerusalem" he adds that this Jerusalem "threatens to collapse like the Waterloo movie scenery" in *The Day of the Locust*. This parodic Jerusalem is not only artificial, but flimsy (317).

5 "Civilized individuality . . . does not want itself, but wants children, wants heirs, wants an estate. Life remains a war against death—civilized man, no more than archaic man, is not strong enough to die—and death is overcome by accumulating time-defying monuments . . ." (286).

6 Brown adds, "Death is overcome on condition that the real actuality of life pass into these immortal and dead things; money is the man; the immortality of an estate or a corporation resides in the dead things which alone endure . . . the last stage of the polis is . . . Nekropolis" (286).

7 In *Classics and Commercials* Edmund Wilson's review of *The Day of the Locust* contains the remark that "the mere aspect of things" in Los Angeles provides "no point d'appui" from which the observer may criticize the setting (55). It may be argued that, in fictional terms, at least, the confusion of museum and mausoleum is a major factor in inducing such disorientation.

8 Huxley also makes his tycoon's financial success largely a personal one, and Stoyte's family background—unlike that of William Randolph Hearst—one

of poverty, of which he is ashamed. Stoyte, a migrant to California from Tennessee, thus resembles far more closely the stereotype of the successful dreamer of the California Dream than did the historical William Randolph Hearst.

9 Keith May has pointed out how even the Los Angeles billboards described in *After Many a Summer*, like the Beverly Pantheon and the paintings in the Stoyte castle-museum, represent allusions to death and aging on the one hand, and to sexuality on the other, which, as May perceptively remarks, are designed to "take the sting out of" both (146).

10 According to Brown, "objects have to be seen as crystallized time in order to be possessed as property; on this point the labor-time theory of value comes closest to psychoanalysis" (276).

11 Even Stoyte's hoarding of art objects represents destructiveness. He entertains a "Tartar's hatred" of the things he collects because they are judged to have market value and hence to confer social prestige. His possessive attitude to his mistress also contains much of this attitude; his "cannibalistic" fondness for her implies a desire to incorporate her into himself which strongly suggests a death-wish against her (45). The destructiveness which Stoyte exemplifies in his person is shown to pervade society through society's acceptance of Stoyte's values.

12 As Irving Malin rightly remarks, in *The Day of the Locust* not only the urban, artificial setting but also nature is "deceptive and brutal" (100). Malin also notes the sense of entrapment and enclosure which characterizes even the natural settings (90).

13 It is perhaps worth noting that Cecilia, Fitzgerald's narrator in *The Last Tycoon*, also employs the imagery of haunting to talk about Hollywood. She sees herself as "a ghost assigned to a haunted house." However, far from rejecting the Hollywood milieu, Cecilia accepts it with "resignation" and is "obstinately unhorrified" (15).

14 In *The Day of the Locust* the destructive violence of the rivalry of Faye's lovers is paralleled by the scene of the cockfight, in which, as Wells has noted, it is the cock named "Brother" (Hermano) which dies (55).

15 Given the debacle that the New Jerusalem of the West has turned out to be, it may well be, as Virgil Lokke has suggested, that Tod's vision of the destruction of Los Angeles is viewed by him as the city's only possible fate: "His plea for the Apocalypse includes no millennium; and there is ample reason for believing that West saw complete social collapse, not as a first act toward social reconstruction, but rather as a last act of mercy" (45).

16 West's working title for *The Day of the Locust* was "The Cheated" (312-13).

17 In *After Many a Summer* the mid-Westerners who end their lives in California further enrich Jo Stoyte through the custom their deaths provide to the Beverly Pantheon (201).

18 Huxley's publishers advertised *After Many a Summer* as his "first novel on the Hollywood scene" (Heard 59).

19 According to a friend, West held the belief that "the people who supposedly worshipped the glamorous stars, really wanted to kill them" out of a sense of deprivation and envy (Martin 304).

20 As David Madden points out, West's very pen-name is ironic: "He did indeed go West, and his life was a play on the many variations of what the West has meant to Americans" (xxi). In *The Day of the Locust*, of course, the focus is on disillusionment with the California Dream.

21 It should be noted that pastiche for Huxley and West as specifically modernist authors, is not a metafictional tool, or a device for calling into question traditional notions of the subjective relations of text and author, but rather functions as an implicit ironic commentary upon the loss of the vitality and the significance of traditional cultural values. As such, the content of the pastiches of verbal styles and literary allusions in *After Many a Summer* and *The Day of the Locust* forms an appropriate part of the contents of Hollywood-Southland's Natural Museum.

22 It is worth comparing *The Day of the Locust* in this respect with another novel of the period with a Hollywood setting, Budd Schulberg's *What Makes Sammy Run?* (1941). In the latter novel, Sammy Glick, described by the novel's narrator as a "predatory genius," is shown on the path to becoming a movie tycoon by practicing the art of "knifing his fellow man in the back" (264, 282). Glick, who supplies the reader with "a blueprint of a way of life that was paying dividends in America in the first half of the twentieth century," is both a potential Charles H. Grotenstein (or, for that matter, a potential Stoyte) and himself one of the "Cheated," whose material success fails to afford him any lasting satisfaction (303, 295). In Schulberg's fictional world the Sammy Glicks are at once the beneficiaries and the victims of the predatory accumulation which motivates the manufacture of the Hollywood dream. In that of *The Day of the Locust* their remoteness, their near-invisibility, enable the reader vicariously to share the bewilderment of the Los Angeles citizens, who—unlike West's narrator, with his hints about "Mr. Kahn a Pleasure-Dome Decreed"—are completely unaware of the social and economic forces which manipulate their responses.

23 Martin points out that in an earlier version of *The Day of the Locust* Tod's vision at this point in the novel included the prophecy that "Only the working classes would resist" the destructive mass movements of the cultists (319).

As Josephine Herbst wrote in 1961, West in his writing (although not in other areas of his political life) "never ventured beyond the accusatory" into specific commitment: "West's concern for the world stopped with a delineation of its dire predicament" (20, 24). In June 1939 West wrote Jack Conroy an account of the reasons for the dichotomy between his very active political life (he worked for the Screen Writers Guild, collected money for Spain, attended meetings of the anti-Nazi League) and the avoidance of specific commitment in fiction: "If I put into 'Day of the Locust' any of the sincere, honest people who work in Hollywood and are making such a great, progressive fight, these chapters couldn't be written satirically and the whole fabric . . . would be badly torn by them." West adds, "I believe that there is a place for the fellow who yells fire and indicates where some smoke is coming from without actually dragging the hose to the spot" (Martin 336). Trachtenberg, who cites West's inability fully to "believe in" Steinbeck's Ma Joad as a credible character, is perhaps correct, however, that in the last assessment West's faith in human nature is strictly limited (187).

24 Propter thinks of money as "secreted" by Stoyte, and of Stoyte as its "personal, human source" (143). To view wealth from this perspective is to overlook the role played by, for example, the migrant workers on the Stoyte estate, in generating it.

25 While Pete Boone's communism is explicitly rejected by the narrator of *After Many a Summer* as dangerously misguided, it is never treated with the fierce ridicule to which Stoyte's ideal of human success is exposed. Stoyte's castle, according to Propter, proclaims to the world that "he's afraid because he's been greedy and domineering" (147). Moreover, the personal qualities of idealism and commitment which Pete's communism has apparently fostered make him a fit disciple for Propter's "philosophic anarchism." Significantly, Pete is the one character in *After Many a Summer* who is shown giving deliberate, conscious assent to Propter's teaching.

26 Of the riot at the film première, Reid comments:

> In Freudian terms, it is the anarchic revolt of a mass id against those 'higher' powers which have denied it and tricked it. In Marxist terms, it is the outrage of victims who have been cynically exploited by a system. In Nietzschean terms, it is the revenge of Dionysian frenzy against a fraudulent Apollonian dream. (154)

That the riot is susceptible of such a variety of readings suggests the complexity of West's vision, but also indicates its lack of a clear-cut diagnosis of the causes of the social malaise his narrator identifies, or of an alternative vision.

27 James F. Light has noted that West, like his character Tod Hackett, frequented the Los Angeles temples and religious cults, including that of Aimee Semple McPherson (153).

James H. Bowden regards Tod's vision as "an adumbrated Revelation . . . the last book in the Christian Scripture, written for reasons of caution to sound futurist" but really aimed at "the Rome of the Neronian persecutions" (287). Although *The Day of the Locust* invites association of its prophetic vision with the carnivorous locusts of Chapter Nine of Revelation, it lacks any notion of the triumph of righteousness, and omits, as Bowden points out, any mention of a heavenly reward, or even of anyone who deserves rewarding. In many respects, then, the vision of *The Day of the Locust* is closer to that of Jeremiah, of the destruction of a corrupt, morally dead Jerusalem, with which Tod himself identifies it, than to the ultimately hopeful vision of Revelation (118).

Chapter Five

Prophets in Babylon

Huxley, West, Armstrong, Steinbeck and Sinclair were all involved in various forms of political activism. Prior to his arrival in the United States in 1937, and throughout 1937 and 1938, Aldous Huxley lectured on pacifism. Nathanael West's involvement with labor disputes, fundraising for victims of the Spanish Civil War, and work with the Anti-Nazi League, are suggestive of the commitments which the Depression, on the one hand, and the worldwide spread of fascism, on the other, might press upon the individual writer. Like Nathanael West, Arnold B. Armstrong was a supporter of the CPUSA-affiliated League of American Writers (Wolfe 169). Steinbeck's journalism on the situation of the California migrants in 1938 was commissioned by the Federal Resettlement Administration (*Letters* 159). This work represented yet one more form of direct political involvement, in this case with the program of the New Deal Democrats.[1] In 1933 Upton Sinclair declared his candidacy for the governorship of California on the Democratic ticket, in the hope of implementing his program to End Poverty in California.

Each of the novels by these writers also reveals the effects of the Depression era, and four of them attempt to address its causes. They do so, however, in the specific socioeconomic conditions of 1930s California. All five novels share a critique, explicit or implicit, of the California Dream and its version of individual possibilities.

A crucial strategy in the presentation of these critiques is the creation of the prophet-figure. Propter, Hackett, Washburn, Casy and the various prophet-figures of *Co-op* are mouthpieces for the authors' denunciations of existing conditions and for the advocacy of utopias.

The influence of Ralph Borsodi upon the ideas presented by Huxley's William Propter, and in particular Propter's conception of the commune, have already been alluded to briefly. Both George Woodcock and Grover Smith have remarked on the extent to which Propter is a mouthpiece for Borsodi's ideas, developed in experimental practice at his "School of Living" in Suffern, New York.[2] An additional, and major, influence on Propter's utopia is that of Huxley's friend, mentor and co-propagandist for pacifism, Gerald Heard. Heard, who first met Huxley in the late 1920s, shortly after the publication of *Point Counter Point*, enjoyed what Heard recalled much later as a "generation of conversation" with him (54, 69). He toured the United States with Huxley to lecture on pacifism. A letter written by Huxley's wife Maria in 1937 records a visit by the two men to a guru, as Maria Huxley wryly comments, "to improve their souls" (Bedford 350). While in California, Heard lived in "a little cell" adjoining a friend's house, to practice meditation. In 1942 he founded a religious community, Trabuco College (371).[3]

A number of aspects of Propter's vision of utopia closely resemble that of Heard in his *Pain, Sex and Time*. Not only Heard's advocacy of the formation of self-sufficient communities as experimental centers for the practice of meditation, which Peter Bowering has noted,[4] but several other elements in Propter's thinking seem to owe a debt to that of Heard. Propter speaks of one possible origin of Stoyte's greed and power hunger in a socioeconomic system which "puts a premium on those qualities," and of bringing into being a system which would discourage their development. Heard writes of a society "founded on an individualism which is made to produce means by appealing to its greed and fear" (222). For Heard, as for Huxley's Propter, the psychological and moral malaise engendered by a particular form of social organization is even more devastating than the economic. The "economic instability" of the existing social system "might be suffered," according to Heard, "if it were not a symptom of a deeper dislocation," of "the competitive and antagonistic manner in which the social system's constituents are functioning . . ." (218). Propter never completely reverses the notion of economic determinism, as Heard does, to argue that a "diseased economics" is the product of "an evil psychology," nor, apparently, does he subscribe to the notion of "spiritual evolution" so central to Heard's thinking.[5] But he does express the belief that, as Heard puts it, "the present system is rooted" in predatory attitudes and behavior, which only an alternative form of social organization would enable individuals to "transcend" (219). Propter praises and experiments with intermediate technology and the self-sufficient commune; Heard invokes Borsodi and advocates a mode of subsistence "completely independent of the present economic system" (218). Like Propter, with his modest expectation that his experimental commune will attract only "a few people" to participate, Heard concedes that his hypothetical community will appeal only to the few.[6] He adds, however, "We do know that the discovery [of the self-transcendence at which both Heard and the fictional Propter aim] can be made, and must be demonstrated" (307). The way to discover, and to demonstrate, for Heard as for Huxley's Propter, is through the self-supporting commune.

In a letter to Kingsley Martin in the summer of 1939, Huxley denied any intention of personally starting a commune, but he continued to be deeply interested in a variety of utopias of community involving economic decentralization and economic self-sufficiency. In 1936, three years before the publication of *After Many a Summer*, he wrote of his intention to "collaborate with Gerald Heard" to develop a utopian synthesis "for free human beings, not a synthesis à la mode de Berlin, Rome or Moscow" (408). In the same month he wrote to Julian Huxley of his interest in the work of Jean Coutrot, as containing "an alternative programme to Marxism" (406-7)[7]. The following year, he agreed with another correspondent that "a complete change in the system of ownership is necessary," but argued that such a change would have little benefit "unless accompanied by decentralization, a reduction of the power of the state, self-government in every activity . . . in a word, anarchism in the sense in which Kropotkin uses the word" (413). In response to a questionnaire circulated by the *Left Review* on writers' stands on the Spanish Civil War, he responded in June 1938 that his sympathies were "of course with the Government side, especially the Anarchists." He added, "Anarchism seems to me much more likely to lead to desirable social change than highly centralized, dictatorial Communism" (423).

In the same letter, in a move that at least one critic has found problematic,[8] he goes on to argue in favor of pacifism. "As for taking sides," he writes, "the choice, it seems to me, is no longer between two users of violence, two systems of dictatorship. Violence and dictatorship cannot produce peace and liberty . . . the necessity of pacifism seems absolutely clear" (423). Propter, too, expresses doubt about the efficacy of violent means to achieve utopian ends, because such means have to be employed "On the strictly human level," that of "greed and fear and hatred, and war and capitalism and dictatorship and slavery" (117). The abolition of "tsardom and capitalism" by violent means, although in itself desirable, led, according to Propter, directly to repressive dictatorship and the crimes of Stalin (113). Propter goes so far as to contend that "most idealism" leads to "war, persecution and mass insanity" (242). The one alternative envisaged to such "idealism"—apart from Stoyte's predatory behavior, or the aimless drifting through life of a Jeremy Pordage or a Virginia Maunciple—is, as Huxley wrote to Kingsley Martin, a quest for spiritual self-transcendence on the margins of society: "Religion can have no politics except the creation of small-scale societies of chosen individuals outside and on the margins of the essentially unviable large-scale societies, whose nature dooms them to self-frustration and suicide" (443).

Huxley's Propter has been described as expressing "Jeffersonian sentiments"; sometimes, with an invitation to make a further comparison between *After Many a Summer* and *The Grapes of Wrath*.[9] If Propter retains something of the "Jeffersonian" ideal, it is the stress on the political significance of guaranteeing the right of private ownership, a concept which the author of *After Many a Summer* finds, however, in Proudhon.[10] In Propter's vision of utopia the desirable distribution of private property is one consistent with "economic security" on the one hand, and with "personal responsibility" on the other. Such equitable distribution should create a situation in which each individual would own enough to escape domination by others, but not enough to dominate in turn (147). This vague formulation fails to address the question of what modes of creating and accumulating private wealth should be set, or indeed who should set the parameters.[11] Propter does, however, echo the distrust expressed in Huxley's letters of the

1930s of both monopoly capitalism and of bureaucratic state socialism in his comparison of Joseph Stalin to Joseph Stoyte (132).[12] The one alternative envisaged by Huxley to domination by either system is that of agrarian self-sufficiency, as practiced by Borsodi.

Nothing could be further from Huxley's reasoned, systematic approach to socioeconomic questions—even to experimentation with mysticism—than the impressionistic subjectivity of Nathanael West's fiction, which depicts North American society in ways which defamiliarize it, revealing its representatives as deformed, but offering no utopian vision, no social or philosophical program, no coherent alternative "system." A further significant difference, in view of the close affinities between Huxley's letters and essays and the pronouncements of the fictional prophet-figure of *After Many a Summer*, is the dichotomy, in the case of West, between the active political commitment of the biographical author and the detached, sardonic and often nihilistic reflections of Tod Hackett.

The biographical West, member of migrant relief committees, of the Anti-Nazi League and the Screen Writers Guild, picketer of department stores and celebrant of the "great, progressive fight" he perceived as being made by Hollywood liberals, bears only the most indirect relationship to the sardonic prophet-figure—and the sardonic narrator—of *The Day of the Locust*.

To make the obvious point that the prophet-figure of *The Day of the Locust* offers no positive utopia—and, moreover, that many of Nathanael West's documented views on contemporary society find no explicit presentation in his fiction—is not to deny a variety of possible, if diffused, intellectual influences upon the constitution of the opinions of Tod Hackett. One of them is surely Spengler, whose theory of the decline of Western civilization is invoked in *A Cool Million*, five years before the publication of *The Day of the Locust*,[13] and which perhaps also informs West's "Burn the Cities," published in 1933.[14] Tod's vision of destruction in *The Day of the Locust* depicts the burning of Los Angeles as "a great bonfire of architectural styles" from Egyptian to Cape Colonial, a bonfire, in other words, of all the cultural traditions epitomizing Western civilization from its beginnings to its decline (184). *The Waste Land* is a further possible source of images of decline.[15] The poem's use of images of debased and trivialized sexuality as an index of that decline—as well as the pastiche of cultural allusions it shares with *The Day of the Locust*—and perhaps the pervasive allusions to Christianity, a force "present by its absence," suggest that these similarities between the Eliot poem and West's novel may be more than coincidental. It is virtually impossible, however, to extract from *The Day of the Locust* any readily paraphrasable set of ideas, let alone a utopia or even any definable "philosophy of life," such as that offered by *After Many a Summer.*

The absence from the novel of a coherent set of values to which the author Nathanael West himself apparently subscribed as a social activist, has led to a good deal of misunderstanding of his work. While Jack Conroy saw in West a "brilliant" satirist, other radically-minded readers dismissed him as a "laughing anarchist," or detected fascistic elements in his work. One critic complained that West depicted Los Angeles without mentioning the growth of "the liberal movement" there (Martin 338, 346). In a letter to Malcolm Cowley of May 1939, West tried to come to terms with the rift between the committed self of that liberal movement and the sardonic *persona* of his fiction: "I'm a comic writer and it seems impossible for me to handle any of the 'big things' without seeming to laugh or at least smile. Is it possible to contrive a right-about face with one's writing because of a conviction based on a theory? I doubt it." West adds, "When not writing a novel—say at a meeting of a committee we have out here to help the migratory worker—I do believe it and try to act on that belief." He had, he told Cowley, "no particular message for a troubled world (except possibly 'beware')" (335-56). The vision of Tod Hackett is, accordingly, drawn more from personal responses to the Southern California scene than from any intellectual heritage, utopian or otherwise.

The negative vision of West's prophet-figure and the author's active political commitment are not, though, as wholly disparate as might at first appear. West's narrator in *The Day of the Locust* satirizes accepted values in order to discredit them, to destroy the illusions that sustain them. Yet the bitter, destructive nay-saying of his comedy suggests a carnivalesque mockery, stemming from the divided desires of a disillusioned idealist. The prophetic vision of destruction in *The Day of the Locust* is linked to the author's political activism by the latter's watchword, "Beware." If Tod Hackett's message resembles a jeremiad, but without any compensating message of hope or redemption, West's work for the Anti-Nazi League or for migrant worker relief committees also represents an attempt to sound a warning, to call others' attention to areas of social crisis.

In his catastrophic, nihilistic vision, Tod Hackett is loosely identified with the historical role, rather than the specific traits or actions, of the Old Testament prophet Jeremiah. Like Jeremiah, he foresees that the disaster about to overtake his society will be the responsibility of that society's members. Yaweh, in Jeremiah's vision, tells the people, "I brought you into a fruitful country, to eat the fruit thereof and the goodness thereof; but when ye entered, ye defiled my land" (Jeremiah 2.7). The mid-Westerners in *The Day of the Locust* similarly enter California's land of plenty only to defile and destroy it. Tod Hackett, like Jeremiah, dwells among false prophets and religious leaders whom the people follow eagerly.[16] If Jeremiah foresees that Jerusalem shall be destroyed but that the gates of the enemy city of Babylon will be "burned with fire" (51:58), Hackett foresees the same fate for the "Jerusalem" of Los Angeles, with the crucial difference that in the latter case the destruction is envisaged as arising from within, whereas Jeremiah sees the destructive forces as both within and without.

Despite these similarities, Hackett is clearly not the righteous individual set apart from the degradation into which his society has fallen, portrayed in the Book of Jeremiah. Hackett wavers between a detached curiosity as to his society's fate, and participation in the destructive impulses which he foresees may destroy it. The name of Jeremiah is invoked in *The Day of the Locust* chiefly as a guarantee of the authenticity of the prophet-figure's vision.

The presentation of the vision, and the character, of Dave Washburn, the prophet-figure of *Parched Earth*, is the product of a marxist-leninist philosophy and of a "proletarian" aesthetic. The latter seems to owe as much to Michael Gold's definition of "Proletarian Realism" in the *New Masses* of September 6, 1930, as it does to the call for "Every proletarian artist" to be a "dialectic materialist," formulated at the Second World Conference of the International Union of Revolutionary Writers in Kharkov, two months later, or to the slogan "socialist realism," which replaced the earlier formula in 1932. As in Gold's aesthetic ideal, *Parched Earth* deals with "real conflicts," struggles between the bourgeoisie and the exploited proletariat. It presents a class struggle that will lead to the victory of the proletariat. It expresses optimism about the eventual outcome of that struggle. It draws on a detailed knowledge of actual work processes in its descriptions of the pitting, cutting and drying of the fruit of the fictional "Tontos Valley."[17] It exhibits the "melodramatic" situations, simplistic characterization and "wish-fulfillment" plot conclusions that Walter Rideout identifies as weaknesses of some proletarian novels of the 1930s.[18] In its stress on the vanguard role played by the Communist Party in class struggle, and in its idealization of the Party's representative in the novel, *Parched Earth* fulfills the contemporary Soviet ideal of the "proletarian novel."[19] And it follows the principles of "socialist realism" in its "photographic" rendering of the details of its subject-matter, an approach based on a naively mimetic conception of literature.[20]

Dave Washburn's background, actions, attitudes and speeches are commensurate with 1930s ideals of a Communist labor leader. Washburn's chief personal trait is courage; he left the IWW when its members "lost their guts," and is the only worker not to panic when the group of evicted workers he leads is attacked by a mob (138, 164). He represents marxism-leninism as a creed of communal action; workers must "stand together." This creed is an egalitarian one which, if it represses ethnic and cultural differences, also calls for mutual respect and solidarity among workers, who are "all the same if they're working men" (191). Washburn organizes cannery workers, fruit pickers and migrants, an indication, perhaps, of the role of the CPUSA in organizing industrial and agricultural workers alike. Washburn's former membership of the IWW links his Communism with an earlier, specifically North American, radical tradition, suggesting that Communism is not to be regarded as an alien political creed, but rather as one that has grown organically from native roots.

In his voicing of revolutionary optimism, his faith that the workers will finally win their "new day," because "All history backs us up," Washburn evokes associations with a Russian rather than an American, historical figure. Like Lenin, Washburn is a sharp-tongued, eloquent orator. Washburn's assurance to his followers of eventual success reads like a crude paraphrase of Lenin's statements of 1913, published on the thirtieth anniversary of Marx's death: "Capitalism has triumphed all over the world, but this triumph is only the prelude to the triumph of labour over capital," and "The Marxist doctrine is omnipotent because it is true" (643, 640).[21] Like Lenin, the fictional Washburn knows that his view is authoritative and that his enemies lack authority, because his analysis is coextensive with history and its laws.

Although the predominant influence on the vision and message of Dave Washburn is clearly that of marxism-leninism, Washburn also derives credibility—or at least borrows credit—from an association, not always consistently developed, with the Old Testament figure of Noah. Although Armstrong's prophet-figure, unlike Noah, has no wife or sons, he fulfills the role assigned to Noah in Genesis: "This same shall comfort us concerning our work and toil of our hands" (5.29). Unlike Hackett/Jeremiah, Washburn's prophecies contain a promise, as well as a warning, a hope for the future as well as a vision of impending doom. Washburn is a conscious, and effective, agent of history. He has found "grace in the eyes of the Lord" (history); he is "a just man" (6. 8-9). He serves as an agent of history's "providence." He takes the future of the working class into a safe refuge from the flood which, as in Genesis, destroys the wicked (the capitalists). After the flood subsides, the members of Washburn's proletarian "family," represented by Hop and Hattie, will be the earth's inheritors, who will be fruitful thereafter and will multiply.

If Washburn's first name suggests a parodic reference to the young warrior of the Book of Samuel who overcame a giant against seemingly impossible odds,[22] the "Wash" of his second name suggests the crucial role he plays as prophet and leader during the flood.[23] "Burn" may be an allusion to the destruction of a corrupt community, that of Sodom, by fire. The name also seems to refer to the washing-away of the curse that lies upon the parched land, monopolized by capitalism. Washburn would thus be a prophet who holds the key, not to Jehovah's plan in history, but to the marxian providential fable.

If marxism-leninism is the major influence on the utopia of *Parched Earth*, it is not without influence on that of *The Grapes of Wrath*. Although Steinbeck, unlike Armstrong, was clearly not a marxist, the question of his relation to the North American Left of the 1930s is at least as important for a reading of *The Grapes of Wrath* and an understanding of its prophet-figure, as more commonly investigated sources.[24] Steinbeck's dialogue with marxism-leninism may be regarded as a product of the socioeconomic crisis of the 1930s. During the Depression years the marxist utopia, as a possible solution to crisis, enjoyed enough popularity among intellectuals to require liberals and conservatives to enter into debate with it, and sometimes to appropriate aspects of it for their own purposes.

Steinbeck himself was a liberal Democrat, a staunch supporter of the New Deal. Those critics, like the anonymous reviewer in *Collier's*, who alleged that *The Grapes of Wrath* was "propaganda for the idea that we ought to trade our system for the Russian system," are clearly mistaken (54). Yet, as other readers have pointed out, the novel owes an unquestionable debt to that product of Depression-era left-wing utopias and aesthetics, the "proletarian novel." As Granville Hicks wrote in *The New Masses* in 1939, *The Grapes of Wrath* was the first work of fiction to give adequate definition to the term "Proletarian Literature" (Robbins 138-43).[25] Michael Gold, in a study of 1941, found in Steinbeck's novel evidence of "a revolution of taste, morals, aspirations and social consciousness" during the 1930s, leading to the development of "a people's culture." It was "not conceivable," according to Gold, that either *The Grapes of Wrath* or Wright's *Native Son* "could have won the same amazing success" in the literary climate of the previous decade (Folsom 245). While rejecting the idea that Steinbeck was in any sense a "proletarian novelist," Walter Rideout, in his *The Radical Novel in the United States*, endorses Gold's view (288).[26] More recently, Sylvia Jenkins Cook has argued that the novel is even "the climax and culmination" of one variety of "left-wing" fiction, drawing upon "use of conventions such as documentary journalism, folk idiom, multiple protagonists, and ideological irony and symbolism that had become common in the thirties in the fiction of other left-wing writers" (Bogardus and Hobson 94-5).

Steinbeck's intellectual engagement with the American Left in the 1930s extended well beyond borrowings of literary technique. If his fiction idealizes the small businessman (the small farmer, the cafeteria or lunch wagon owner in *The Grapes of Wrath* or *In Dubious Battle*),[27] there is common ground in the Left's attack on monopoly capitalism and the bitter attacks of his narrator in *The Grapes of Wrath* on the "great owners," one of them clearly based on William Randolph Hearst. Steinbeck alluded to Hearst in unflattering terms in a letter of 1933, where Hearst is described as "fouling up the planet" (66). In *The Grapes of Wrath* the migrants talk about a California landowner, a "newspaper fella near the coast, got a million acres. . . . Fat, sof' fella with little mean eyes an' a mouth like a ass-hole" (226). Such critical attacks are an essential aspect of Steinbeck's Jeffersonianism; individual industry is fulfilling for the entrepreneur and socially useful, while accumulation of property to the point where the owner can have no immediate and personal relation to it endangers both the owner and society as a whole. However, as Owens has pointed out, *The Grapes of Wrath* also suggests that Jefferson's agrarianism as a social philosophy suffers from a number of inadequacies which Jim Casy's utopia of mutuality and community is designed to remedy[28] (132-33). It would clearly be an exaggeration to equate the utopia of mutual cooperation of *The Grapes of Wrath*, and its basis in a Whitmanian view, with the class-conscious dialectical materialism of marxism-leninism. Yet the two utopias share a condemnation of the predatory attitudes and behavior perceived as stemming from unbridled monopoly capitalism.

According to Jackson J. Benson, Steinbeck was acquainted with a number of prominent California Communists during the 1930s, although he was apparently deeply disturbed by an invitation from Anna Louise Strong to join the Party (424-45), and he tenaciously fought any attempt to give his fiction "the communist angle" (*Letters* 174). Despite a remark in a letter to Mavis McIntosh, that, "There are as many communist systems as there are communists," he stereotyped Communists as possessing personal traits which he regarded with a mixture of dislike and admiration (107). "I dislike them as people," he wrote to Louis Paul in the year that he published *In Dubious Battle* (1936), "I rather imagine the apostles had the same waspish qualities. . . ." He adds, however, "But that dislike is personal . . . and some of these communist field workers are strong, pure, inhumanly virtuous men. Maybe that's another reason I personally dislike them and that does not redound to my credit" (120). Although he resisted identification with the marxist-leninist utopia itself, he apparently found enough in it to engage sympathetically to remark, à propos of the CPUSA, "If the fools would only change the name from Communist to, say, American Liberty party, their principles would probably be embraced overnight" (108).

Not surprisingly, then, *The Grapes of Wrath* offers evidence of a dialogue with marxist and marxist-leninist ideas, and parallels to passages in *Capital*, I. If the similarity is more than coincidental, if it does indeed supply evidence of an engagement with marxism, it is an engagement which, as in the case of his use of Christianity, has resulted in a total appropriation for Steinbeck's own purposes. The narrator's discussion in *The Grapes of Wrath* of the role of the political leader is a case in point. His repeated assertion that labor movements and the rise of leaders are a matter of "results, not causes," illustrates both the implicit allusion to an economic-determinist concept of the leader's role and its appropriation to serve a very different conception of the dynamics of social change (163-66). The causes of such change, according to Steinbeck's narrator, "lie deep and simple." The narrator's careful tracing of changes in landholding patterns and of agricultural methods in Oklahoma and California of the 1930s makes clear that the emergence of a response such as Casy's is linked to changes in the mode of production. Yet most individuals do not respond as Casy does. Moreover, Steinbeck's narrator appears to be less concerned with general conditions constituting causal agents of revolutionary or potentially revolutionary situations than with more immediate, more subjective generators of unrest: "a hunger in a stomach, multiplied a million times." There is emphasis, too, on individual psychological as well as physical needs: "hunger in a single soul, hunger for joy and some security" (164). The narrator's conception of political leaders as "results, not causes" is further complicated by the Steinbeckian idea of the "phalanx," a spontaneous collective movement of individuals acting with a single mind and will. Social progress, in *The Grapes of Wrath*, is a matter of individual and collective psychological impulses, of a "stumbling-forward ache," of willingness to "die for a concept" (164). The conception of a collective desire which leads, however falteringly, in the direction of social progress, makes of that progress a matter of "group mind," as much as it is a product of socioeconomic change.

A second area in which the narrator's commentary in *The Grapes of Wrath* appears to owe something to marxist ideas is in the discussion of the relation of labor and ownership. Marx's statement in *Capital* that human labor "acts upon external nature" in ways that transform the human beings performing the labor seems to lie behind the narrator's discussion of the part played by labor in validating ownership: "That's what makes the land ours—being born on it, working on it, dying on it. That makes ownership, not a paper with numbers on it" (35). In Marx, however, control of the means of production (by a self-employed artisan, for instance, as opposed to a capitalist employing others) does not necessarily alter the general character of the production. In *Capital*, moreover, Marx initially considers the labor process in isolation from "any specific social formation," before moving on to discuss the production of surplus value under capitalism (283). In *The Grapes of Wrath*, the question of control of the means of production is treated as crucial not only in relation to the question of economic exploitation, but also for the "spiritual" value the narrator sets on emotional ties to the means of production (38).

Much of the support for the claim that Steinbeck's narrator engages and appropriates marxist ideas is to be found in Chapter Fourteen, where the narrator warns of the potential for social revolution represented by the distress and discontent of the migrants. In this chapter, Steinbeck's narrator appears to allude to the statement in *Capital* where Marx differentiates human from animal "labor" by the conscious preconception of design peculiar to human work activity:

> What distinguishes the worst architect from the best of bees is that the architect builds the cell in his mind before he constructs it in wax. At the end of every labour process, a result emerges which had already been conceived by the worker at the beginning, hence already existed ideally. Man not only effects a change of form in the materials of nature; he also realizes . . . his own purpose in those materials. (284)

Steinbeck's narrator comments on "the last clear definite function of man—muscles aching to work, minds aching to create beyond the single need":

> To build a wall . . . and in the wall . . . to put something of Manself, and to Manself take back something of the wall . . . to take hard muscles from the lifting, to take the clear lines and form from conceiving. For man, unlike any other thing . . . in the universe, grows beyond his work, walks up the stairs of his concepts, emerges ahead of his accomplishments. (164)

This passage appears to parallel the statement in Marx in at least two respects: in its emphasis on the twofold transformation of materials and producers in the labor process, and in its insistence on the capacity for prior conception as the distinguishing mark of human labor. In Marx these formulations lead on to further analysis of the changing functions of use values in the labor process, and thence to a discussion of the labor theory of value. In Steinbeck's text the narrator's statement modulates from a discussion of the nature of human labor to one of the nature of human *achievement*, and thence to a *credo*, an affirmative declaration of faith in human collective instinct and human potential for progress. "Man" is capable of growing "beyond his work," of emerging "ahead of his accomplishments."

The narrator's *credo* continues with a celebration of the progress that may arise out of violent conflict, including class conflict; an assertion that the oppressor's brutality itself gives evidence of a striving toward betterment: "If the step were not being taken, if the stumbling-forward ache were not alive, the bombs would not fall, the throats would not be cut" (164). It is possible to detect here an implicit allusion to, perhaps a parodic reversal of, the title of Lenin's attack on opportunism among the Russian Social Democrats, *One Step Forward, Two Steps Back*. Lenin's work ends with a statement of faith in the inevitability of human progress, couched in marxist terms: "One step forward, two steps back. . . . It happens in the lives of individuals, and it happens in the history of nations and the development of parties." It would be "the most criminal cowardice," Lenin asserts, to "doubt even for a moment the inevitable and complete triumph of the principles of revolutionary Social-Democracy . . ." (414). Lenin assures his readers that the proletariat will "more and more firmly close its ranks," despite "all zigzags and backward steps" (415). This makes for interesting comparison with the words of Steinbeck's narrator: "Having stepped forward, he may slip back, but only half a step, never the full step back . . . every little beaten strike is proof that the step is being taken" (164). Jim Casy, as prophet-figure, becomes the eventual spokesperson for a view of human progress as a matter of faltering (but never wholly reversed) steps taken, not by a single class, but by humanity: "ever' time they's a little step fo'ward, she may slip back a little, but she never slips clear back" (425).

Unlike Lenin's proletariat, the striking migrant workers in *The Grapes of Wrath* confront "the great owners" in an assertion of claims to economic "justice" within the existing economic system. If their destitution and displacement have the potential, as Casy claims, to "change the whole country," they themselves are not consciously radicals (190). Steinbeck's narrator seems, in fact, to employ allusions to marxism and to leninism, not to support a revolutionary movement toward the overthrow of the capitalist state and a dictatorship of the proletariat, but rather in support of Casy's utopia of cooperation. It is not the militant proletariat that Steinbeck's narrator celebrates in Chapter Fourteen of *The Grapes of Wrath*, but "Manself," the human collective instinct for progress. Steinbeck's narrator, then, quite as much as Huxley's narrator and prophet-figure in *After Many a Summer*, finds it necessary as part of a response to the utopian solutions to socioeconomic crisis offered in the Depression years, to engage the marxist-leninist utopia. He finds it rewarding to do so purely upon his own terms.

Steinbeck's prophet owes more to the central figure of the Gospels than to any marxian original. Despite the difficulties of critics in defining Casy's identity, and his relation to Tom Joad in terms of New Testament analogies, difficulties which have occasionally led them to "the outskirts of baffled imbecility,"[29] there seems little doubt that Casy's prophetic role is that of a Christ-figure (171). It is also a measure of Steinbeck's sympathetic identification with the Left that, not for the first time in his fiction, he makes his Christ-figure a radical labor leader.

Steinbeck's use of religious analogies in developing labor leader characters predates *The Grapes of Wrath* by at least five years. In a short story, "The Raid" (1934), two Communist labor leaders are beaten by vigilantes. Steinbeck's account is reminiscent of stories of Christian martyrdom. One of the organizers tells his persecutors, in an echo of Christ's words, and a prefiguring of Jim Casy's, "We're doing it for you. . . . You don't know what you're doing"

(107). Religious, specifically Christian evangelist, overtones are also apparent in the portrayal of the young Communist labor organizer, Jim Nolan, in *In Dubious Battle*. His co-worker sees in his militant dedication to the cause of marxism, "something religious" (200). Nolan and his comrades are "Partakers of the blood of the Lamb" (254).

Casy, while at once more religious (although unorthodox) than Root or Nolan, and less self-righteous than Nolan, like them borrows the poetic authority of association with the figure of Christ. Furthermore, while Root and Nolan are identified as religious "disciples" only in the most general terms, the serious parody of Christ in the figure of Casy is easily discernible and consistently developed.

Before the publication of *Co-op* in 1936, Sinclair had supported the U.S. Socialist Party for three decades by his writings and other political activities. He had run for Congress on the Socialist ticket three times, and twice for the governorship of California. Through his pamphlets and fiction, and the various protests and demonstrations in which he had been involved, from the free speech fights in the years after World War I to the campaign to free Tom Mooney, Sinclair was one of the best-known popularizers of socialism in North America. As the change of his voter registration in 1933 indicates, Sinclair seems to have experienced doubts as to the practicability of winning converts to socialism within any movement retaining the stigma of the term. As his character Sigvald Soren points out, "Names make a lot of difference" (319). According to Soren, for North Americans the word "socialism" carries connotations of a "foreign" and "atheistic" system, "all mixed up with free love, and drinking beer, and whatnot" (42-3). However, as Sinclair's narrator in *Co-op* recognizes, the term "production for use," which Sinclair adopted during the 1934 gubernatorial race to describe his program of cooperatives for the unemployed, had also acquired thoroughly negative connotations, through the smear campaign organized against EPIC. Soren therefore suggests that the cooperative members refer to their cooperative movement as one of "reciprocal economy."[30]

The cooperative movement as a whole, like the coalition of radicals and liberals which composed the EPIC movement of 1934, is eclectic, and tolerant of individuals' divergent beliefs. The members of the San Sebastian Self-Help Exchange resolve to "have nothing to do with politics" in the daily running of their cooperative. They agree not to ask members about "race . . . creed or . . . party" (84). However, the majority of the Self-Help Exchange members, like California's cooperatives in the 1934 gubernatorial race, are supporters of EPIC: "The Self-Help Exchange was EPIC in action, and people who were living EPIC voted it automatically" (375).[31] The purpose of the Self-Help Exchange, apart from saving the unemployed from starvation, is to serve as an example of socialism in action to a society which fears the idea of "socialism," but has little realistic conception of what form socialism might take within the American social context.

Despite the eclectic nature of the cooperative movement, the utterances of its prophet-figures make clear that the cooperative socialist utopia forms an integral part of the movement. The San Sebastian Self-Help Exchange's largest financial backer at the Exchange's founding is a Socialist, the wealthy Mabel Saugus (66). The cooperative is joined by a founder member of the Llano colony, who speaks of the socialist "dream" that "some day human beings will learn to cooperate, instead of fighting each other" (49). Charlie Day and Sigvald Soren are both influenced by socialism. Day has "picked up" the idea of the Self-Help Exchange from contact with "an old Socialist" (25). Soren is attracted by the socialist utopia's apparent compatibility with pacifism (38, 42).

Soren's emphasis on a gradual, peaceful transition to socialism is paralleled in an EPIC pamphlet of 1934, in which Sinclair defines a Socialist as "a man who believes that necessary social changes can be brought about by democratic action of the people at the ballot box" (*Lie Factory* 18).

While the dominant influences on the ideas of the prophet-figures in *Co-op* are clearly those of socialism and of European cooperative movements, a number of specifically North American influences are also apparent. Charlie Day expresses a vision of citizens "organizing to take their country away from exploiters and build a new co-operative industry," but also of utilizing the full potential of currently under-exploited technology. His dream of "harnessing the forces of nature" to create "leisure for everybody" through nationalization of industry seems to owe something to Bellamy's *Looking Backward*—[32] though Day's utopian vision contains no hint of the regimentation of citizens' labor during their brief period in the workforce, which is central to *Looking Backward*. Descriptions of the Self-Help Exchange also reveal an evident debt, as did Sinclair's EPIC program, to the practical example set by the existing cooperative movement in California. In his autobiography, Sinclair places on historical record the story of three dwellers in "Pipe City," Oakland, a cluster of empty drainpipes where homeless people congregated. Endowed with "education and business experience," these men founded a financially successful cooperative. According to Sinclair, this organization was both the model for the fictional Self-Help Exchange of *Co-op* and an example to the social experimenters who subsequently founded "two or three hundred" similar organizations during the Depression years (*Autobiography* 280-81). As in Sinclair's novel, the members of the loose-knit California cooperative movement found in the EPIC program a theoretical exposition of the principles of "production for use" on which their cooperatives were founded (*Autobiography* 271).

The prophet-figures of *Co-op* vary in the degree to which they parody a biblical or religious original. Charlie Day is an inspired social visionary, but, strictly speaking, not a "prophet-figure" in the parodic sense that Propter, Casy, Hackett, or Prosser and Soren are prophet-figures. The Reverend Prosser's given name, Elias, is a variant of "Elijah." The name identifies Prosser with the Biblical prophet who defied the wicked ruler, Ahab, and denounced the worship of false gods. Elijah is the prophet whose "mantle" Sinclair claimed, figuratively speaking, for his own calling as a utopian "evangelist." Prosser's first name further identifies him with Elijah's successor, Elisha, who fed a hungry multitude and brought healing to a land stricken by famine. Both Elijah and Elisha were wanderers who, like Elias Prosser, survived on gifts provided by their followers.

If Prosser parodies prophet-figures of the Old Testament, Sigvald Soren is explicitly associated with an evangelist of the New. Like Saint Paul, Soren writes "epistles" to his followers when he is away from them: "Stick to the co-op . . . Come to the meetings. Lay everything on the table. Be fair to one another. Help all your fellow members. Do your work honestly and have faith in our cause." If the members continue in this course, Soren assures them, "everything that is good and worthwhile" will come to them (300). These words are explicitly paralleled in *Co-op* with Romans, 12. A cooperative member is prompted, by Soren's contribution to the "co-op" newsletter, to open his Bible at the words of Paul: "Be kindly affectioned one to another . . . not slothful in business; fervent in spirit; serving the Lord . . ." (301). As a lobbyist for EPIC in Washington, Soren arms himself for an approaching battle with an unsympathetic bureaucrat "in the ancient Biblical style." The narrator applies to Soren Paul's words to the Ephesians: "For we wrestle not against flesh and blood, but against principalities, against powers, against the rulers of the darkness of this world" (395). Thus Soren is portrayed as, like Paul, a militant evangelist of a utopian "gospel" who struggles against intangible forces of tyranny and evil for the triumph of his creed.

The prophet-figures draw their credibility and authority, the guarantees of the authenticity of their visions, from other sources besides the parodying of religious originals. Each prophet-figure shares the status accorded the traditional stereotype of a particular profession: university teacher, artist, labor leader, preacher, seaman, business executive. All but one of the prophets are also presented in a highly idealized light. All of them are shown as possessing special understanding of, and sensitivity to, society's plight, although the type of sensitivity is different in each prophet's case. Moreover, three prophet-figures, while in large measure deriving their prestige from association with a particular religious tradition, are presented as capable of calling that tradition into question, thereby affirming the superiority of their own visions.

William Propter is, as suggested earlier, a version of the guru. In fact his chosen profession places him squarely in the category of those unorthodox religious teachers, instructors in brain breathing and preachers of various forms of asceticism, who are satirized in *The Day of the Locust*. Possibly this is one reason why a clearly bogus guru, Swami Yogalinga of the School of Personality, makes a fleeting appearance in *After Many a Summer*, as if to distance Propter, by means of contrast, from the cranks and charlatans of Los Angeles, and endow him with a greater air of authenticity. Any impulse to ridicule on the reader's part is further counteracted by allusions to Propter's past as a university teacher, a profession that confers on him a certain intellectual respectability.

Tod Hackett derives professional authority and credibility from his status as an artist. His antecedents are to be found among various literary portraits of the suffering artist in the Romantic and post-Romantic traditions. The Stephen Daedalus of *Ulysses*, with his religious apostasy, self-doubt, preoccupation with his artist's identity, curiosity about the less salubrious areas of his city, springs to mind, as does the mocking and tormented observer of urban life in *Le Spleen de Paris*.[33] West's own Miss Lonelyhearts, although he parodies Jesus, not Jeremiah, is another likely forerunner of Tod Hackett, and there are affinities with the introverted anti-hero of "Prufrock." Another possible influence on Hackett is the character of Gumbril in Huxley's *Antic Hay*, a novel to which, as Randall Reid has pointed out, West's fiction almost certainly owes a good deal.[34] Both Hackett and Gumbril are sensitive young men at the start of their careers. Both are unassertive, and unimpressive in physical appearance. Both are engaged in a quest for values, which is represented in each novel by a meditation on a piece of music. Like Hackett, Gumbril at one point in the novel conceives of himself as resembling a prophet (60). Like others in the tradition of the suffering artist and prophet, Hackett experiences his awareness of society's malaise as a source of private pain. His first name in German means "death," which, in the absence of a utopian alternative to the *status quo*, is all that he can foretell.

Armstrong's Dave Washburn is a characteristic example of the labor leader as hero commonly found in radical fiction of the 1930s. Whether or not there is any direct influence from earlier novels, the character of Washburn clearly has affinities with that of Fer, in Mary Heaton Vorse's *Strike!* (1930), or with that of Amos Freer in Fielding Burke's *Call Home the Heart* (1932). Fer, although a less confident leader than Washburn—at one point in Vorse's novel he is described as "a burdened anxious boy"—is, like Washburn, able to captivate an audience (57). The workers regard Fer as a prophet, as a "Messiah" (57). He is "their David defying the Goliath of the mills" (176). Like Washburn, he lives with the workers, sharing their hardships. Washburn, like both Fer and Freer, is portrayed as possessing qualities of forthrightness, practicality and common-sense. It is Washburn's ability to know, like Freer, "what to do," that gives him his authority and credibility in the narrator's eyes (310). Like other field organizers in the proletarian tradition, Washburn is distinguished not by his theoretical grasp of the fine points of marxist-leninist doctrine, but by his ability to deliver others from their predicament by practical leadership. It is for this ability to take action, in accordance with the inevitable course of history, but also toward the righting of specific labor grievances, that the narrator asks the reader to admire him.

Jim Casy is, of course, an ex-preacher as well as a labor leader, and as such is endowed with some of the status attaching to both professions. This combination of preacher and labor leader is not unprecedented in the fiction of the 1930s, any more than in documented historical incident. Vorse's *Strike!* for example, features Brother Williams, a preacher who leads the striking textile workers of Gastonia in a prayer in which he likens them to the children of Israel in bondage, and calls upon God to "hear them in their struggle" (89). In Robert Cantwell's *The Land of Plenty* (1934), strikers in flight from the police are helped by a sympathetic preacher. Casy, with his religious intuitions and belief in an oversoul, clearly owes as much to this tradition of the religious sympathizer with labor agitation as he does to that of Fer, Freer and Washburn.

Further influences on the figure of Casy seem to be those of Barney Graham and Joe Hill, labor leaders killed in the workers' cause whom ballads present as crucified and resurrected Christ figures. Just as in "I saw Joe Hill the Other Night," Joe Hill assures the dreamer that his spirit lives on "where working men defend their rights," so in *The Grapes of Wrath* the spirit of the murdered leader Jim Casy passes, figuratively speaking, to Tom Joad and to other believers in Casy's message. From this ballad tradition, then, Casy inherits not only the prestige of the heroic labor leader, but that of the murdered labor leader as a risen Christ.

Charlie Day represents the American businessman who, when the capitalist system has failed him, seeks cooperative alternatives. Homeless and destitute, reduced to camping out in "Pipe City," he develops a plan for his economic salvation, and that of others. The portrayal of Day is as stereotyped as that of Propter or of Soren. Day epitomizes the aggressively efficient executive, even when his abilities are cooperatively directed. He is a "driving force" of the Self-Help Exchange, "one to tackle any job," an organizer, under whose chairmanship a meeting proceeds as if "rehearsed" (135).

Day suggests where offices can be found, organizes the cooperative's work by "sections," draws up lists of new members, presides over the discussion of grievances (55, 63, 66-7, 192). Herbert Alding, the young New Deal bureaucrat who visits San Sebastian to study the Self-Help Exchange, recognizes him immediately as "one you could deal with" (257). Elias Prosser, an ordained minister and an itinerant preacher, represents the involvement of the church in the cooperative movement. He conveys the authority of his calling in his preaching of the "message" of EPIC. Prosser delivers his message of cooperation with "old-time gospel fervour," the "delivery and emotional equipment" of the evangelist (222-23). Sigvald Soren, the unemployed manual worker, has been a traveling casual laborer, in the manner of Dave Washburn or Jim Casy. Like Washburn, he has traveled across the country, living by his work and his wits. Like Casy, he has been in jail. He has worked as sailor, miner, farmer, trucker. Soren represents the narrator's stereotype of the American working-class, of that class's alleged resilience, resourcefulness, good-humor and common-sense, and its skill in practical psychology (81). Thus the prophet-figures of *Co-op* present a cross-section of American social classes—business executive, clerical professional man, manual worker—in keeping with the multi-class political constituency of the cooperative movement. By dividing the functions of the prophet-figures among several individuals, the novel democratizes those functions. Each member or supporter of the Self-Help Exchange is potentially a prophet-figure in his or her own right.

The novels' narrators function as dramatized representatives of the author, and as ideological adjudicators for him. It is hardly surprising, therefore, that the prophet-figures who preach utopian messages are presented by their narrators with unqualified approval. Propter, for instance, is idealized in the description of his physical appearance. He has the face of a statue on a cathedral, with "deeply shadowed folds and hollows . . . rough-hewn so as to be expressive even at a distance." It is a face "expressive of sensibility and intelligence as well as of power, of a gentle and humorous serenity" (18). Propter is generous and patient with the migrants, comprehending of Jo Stoyte's neuroses, gently satirical of Jeremy Pordage (but never malicious), and endlessly willing to explain to others his vision of the truth. His other distinguishing feature is one he shares with virtually all Huxley's religious heroes—an ability to hold other characters motionless and nearly silent for pages on end, while he lectures them on religious transcendence and social reform. If readers have often labeled Propter "a gasbag," it is the narrator's lack of critical distance from him that largely accounts for this impression.[35] Dave Washburn, a less fully-realized character than Propter, is likewise presented solely in terms suggestive of the narrator's unconditional approval. If his preaching of a marxist utopia meets with setbacks, if those to whom he advocates solidarity laugh at him, or fail to stand firm at the factory gate, the fault lies not with Washburn but with the false consciousness and lack of courage of those whom he seeks to organize. Washburn, on the other hand, is presented as the ideal Communist, a moral and ideological norm for others. Even Jim Casy, although he admits to more human frailties and greater uncertainty about the correctness of his vision than Propter or Washburn exhibit,[36] is nonetheless "a man that's baptized," as Ma Joad calls him, unusually sensitive, altruistic and courageous (101). In keeping with his image of efficient organizer, Charlie Day of *Co-op* is "well-built" and "vigorous" in appearance (48). The Reverend Prosser corresponds closely to the stereotype of a religious ascetic, with his "sharp and prematurely wrinkled face, full of earnestness and zeal" (218). Sigvald Soren is physically impressive in a different way. Six feet tall, with a "barrel" chest and "powerful" arms, he looks like "the grandson of all the Vikings" (38, 41). He has too, an improbably saintly character. He is kindly, patient, tolerant, generous, shrewd, and apparently incapable of losing his temper (38, 42, 81, 388-413). Each of the prophet-figures is presented as one of the most astute and perceptive members of his society, capable of registering the social, economic or moral climate, and any changes that are judged to be taking place. It is on the credibility of this presentation that the authority of each prophet-figure ultimately rests.

In each case, the prophet-figure's power of vision is set in paradoxical contrast to his lack of worldly success. All the prophet-figures are men of humble background, who pursue their prophetic vocations in obscurity. Propter, although he has a modest private income, apparently once attended public school with Jo Stoyte, during the latter's years of poverty. Propter is despised by the

Stoytes of the world for his lack of worldly ambition, snubbed by the photographers at a college ceremony, who turn away from him "contemptuously" in their quest for celebrities (291). What little renown he enjoyed as the author of *Short Studies in the Counter Reformation*, Propter has renounced in favor of agriculture and solitary meditation. Tod Hackett, although middle-class and Yale-educated, is a $30-a-week screen designer, who lives in one room on Hollywood Boulevard. Dave Washburn, like many of those he leads, is a penniless hobo. Casy, although he receives some of the respect accorded by rural Oklahomans to a preacher, is equally destitute, and does not even enjoy the protection of the law. Of the prophet-figures in *Co-op*, Charlie Day has lost all his wealth in the Depression and has been reduced to destitution. The Reverend Prosser lives in voluntary poverty, supporting himself and his wife through donations and the bartering of EPIC literature for food and gasoline (219, 223). Soren has struggled his whole life to earn a subsistence income, having once been driven to steal to stay alive.

The success of the prophets as evangelists, if judged by the number of their followers, is not remarkable, either. William Propter wins one convert (who is killed even before he has the chance to tell Propter of his conversion) and has an embryonic commune maintained by a handful of people. Tod Hackett presents a vision in the form of a painting to which others may, or may not, have responded. Washburn leads a ragtag group of workers who cannot even mount a successful demonstration. Casy is murdered before he has been able to communicate his message to more than a few. Because of the prophet-figures' sensitivity to social, economic and moral conditions, however, the reader is urged to attend to their voices.

The prophet-figures in *Co-op* achieve more success than Propter, Hackett, Washburn or Casy. Charlie Day organizes a thriving cooperative. The Reverend Prosser wins converts to the EPIC movement in San Sebastian, inspiring the founding of the town's first "EPIC club." Soren takes part in the founding of the Self-Help Exchange, wins the support of wealthy benefactors for the cooperative, and campaigns effectively for EPIC. As the San Sebastian Self-Help Exchange's representative in Washington, he succeeds, against all odds, in securing an interview with

Roosevelt—an interview on which, the narrator makes clear, the fate of the cooperative utopia in California will ultimately depend (415).

Although each prophet-figure is credited with vision, the particular type of insight varies in each case. Huxley's Propter both practices meditation and preaches on the basis of his observations of society. He is shown as entering altered states of consciousness by means of meditation. Yet the utopia he preaches is explained to others in broad generalizations that seem to be derived from intellectual analysis rather than from suprarational, supralinguistic experience. West's Tod Hackett, on the other hand, is an intuitive artist whose understanding of the imminent doom develops through subjective perception. For him art is a mode of exploration as well as expression. The vision finally synthesized in the image of the holiday crowd burning Los Angeles is also arrived at through social observation, in Hackett's studies of the city's "Dancers" and "Starers," its worshippers and cultists. The central image of the burning of Los Angeles thus assumes greater detail and clarity as the narrative progresses, through the use of Tod's artistic soundings.[37] The marxist vision of Armstrong's Dave Washburn is perhaps the only one of the four which takes as its basis, without alteration or appropriation, an entire pre-existent thought system. Washburn has no need of intuition, nor of the rationality of a Propter. He struggles against the power of capital in the knowledge that his cause cannot fail because he works in accordance with the laws of history. His vision derives from an apparently simple hermeneutical operation, the interpretation of a marxist system that presumably interprets itself. Steinbeck's Jim Casy, on the other hand, not unlike Tod Hackett, proceeds to his vision through a blend of intuition and social observation that offers him no pre-formulated assurances. Casy finds himself constantly testing new positions. Even on the night of his death, when he has already become a strike leader and a prophetic teacher to Tom Joad, Casy still maintains, "I ain't got it worked out yet" (422). As a sensitive antenna of the migrant phalanx he registers changes in the social climate. He is able, as he says, to "hear the way folks are feelin'" (275). Before the Joads have even reached California, he expresses his sense of "restlessness" among the migrating people (190). Unlike Hackett, he finds his intuitive conclusions corroborated by those of others, notably Tom Joad (275). In his prophetic intuition of social change Casy is, as he says, one who "climbs fences that ain't even strung up yet" (191). Sinclair's prophet-figures are visionaries who arrive at their utopian visions, not through intuition, but by the exercise of practical reasoning. Charlie Day develops his plan of founding a Self-Help Exchange after reading socialist literature in the public library. For Day, the cooperative consists of "A group of men doing useful things" they could not accomplish as individuals (25, 27). The Reverend Elias Prosser is both a "well-grounded economist" and a "political tactician," well-accustomed to addressing skeptical, independent-minded audiences (223). Sigvald Soren views his role in the establishment of the cooperative utopia as that of a simple coordinator of those who need someone "to show them how" and "help them get a start" (43). Among his chief concerns are the establishment of "an exact accounting system," the avoidance of conflict with local capitalists, and the setting up of committees (52, 60, 67). Like Day and Prosser, Soren is presented as a practical visionary, whose plans are not general theories, but minutely realizable concrete plans.

The prophet-figures derive their prophetic authority from the parodying of respected figures, from idealized presentation of their characters, and from references to their prophetic gifts. A further point of common ground is the authoritative perspective from which they critique or endorse traditional Christian belief.

Huxley, West, Armstrong, Steinbeck and Sinclair all function within the context of a post-Christian universe of discourse, in which Christian doctrine and ethical systems are viewed as exhausted and surpassed. Their prophet-figures derive prestige, and authority for their utopian or catastrophic social messages, from addressing the vacuum left by this decline in traditional religious belief or, as in the case of Sinclair, by appropriating that belief for the preaching of a social message. Propter, for instance, rejects the notion of a "personal God, dispenser of forgiveness"; faith in an after life of rewards and punishments; faith in "the absolute reality of human personalities," as well as in any "single inspired book"; in churches, priests or sacraments. Such erroneous beliefs, Propter considers, are obstacles in the way of self-transcendence. Propter's skepticism about institutionalized religion of any kind is unqualified. It is in keeping with his post-Christian alternative to institutionalized Christianity that the only "believers" exempted from his critique are Christian mystics (98, 290).

In the case of Tod Hackett, reflection on the bankruptcy of traditional belief leads not to the attempt to formulate a new philosophical system, but to a heightened sense of doom. Hackett has studied the cults of Los Angeles with which the retired mid-Westerners attempt to replace their lost faith in the religion of their fathers, and knows them to offer no solution. Hackett's attitude to traditional Christianity is made clear by his thoughts as he listens to the Bach chorale, "Come Redeemer, Our Saviour." "If there was a hint of a threat," in the music, (Hackett asks himself), "and a tiny bit of impatience, could Bach be blamed? After all, when he wrote this music the world had already been waiting for its lover more than seventeen hundred years" (129). The music, in Hackett's interpretation of it, ends with a statement. "'Come or don't come,' the music seemed to say, 'I love you and my love is enough.'" If Christ hears this moving statement, the narrator concludes sardonically, "He gave no signs." In Hackett's world the only message a prophet can offer is one of destruction, without hope of redemption; his only relation to faith can be a cry against the cultists and false religious leaders who delude their followers (184).

Dave Washburn never alludes to religion in any way. Indeed, for a small rural community in the early 1930s, Caldwell as a whole seems surprisingly indifferent to religious observances. The religious associations of Washburn with Noah, for example, are entirely appropriated for non-religious purposes. No explicit debate with Christian belief arises, therefore; although one may surmise that Washburn, as a former Wobbly, shares the Wobblies' satirical attitude toward organized religion, and their gibes of the "You'll have pie in the sky when you die" variety at the churches' delusory promises of future compensation for present suffering.

Casy makes his critique of Christianity explicitly, as he reflects on the needs of the Oklahomans about to set out on the road to California: "Hope of heaven when their lives ain't lived? Holy Sperit when their own sperit is downcast and sad? They got to live before they can afford to die" (56). Casy also rejects the concepts of sin and atonement: "There ain't no sin and there ain't no virtue. There's just stuff people do." In his own mind, though, Casy's most heretical conviction, that because of which he "can't be a preacher no more," is his discovery of the "one big soul." If it is true, Casy argues, in a final rejection of the orthodox transcendent and yet providential deity, that "the human sperit" and "the Holy Sperit" are one, then "Why do we got to hang it on God or Jesus?" (24). It is his Whitmanian faith in a relational view of consciousness, self and deity that shapes Casy's attitude to humanity: "Gonna lay in the grass, open an' honest with anybody that'll have me. Gonna cuss an' swear an' hear the poetry of folks talkin'. All that's holy . . ." (102). Like Hackett and Washburn, Casy rejects traditional Christian doctrine as inadequate to human psychic and social needs. Like Propter, he evolves his own post-Christian religious and ethical system, based on immediate personal experience.

Only the narrator of *Co-op* adopts a tone of respect, rather than of critical skepticism, toward orthodox Christianity.[38] Given the efforts of Sinclair's political opponents to brand him an atheist during the 1934 EPIC campaign, it is hardly surprising that *Co-op*, written to promote the ideals of EPIC in fictional form, should emphasize the possibility of harmony, rather than conflict, between the cooperative movement and Christian institutions and beliefs. Indeed, throughout his literary career, Sinclair's writings stressed the idea of the founding of a Socialist utopia as a fulfillment of the Christian gospel, and of participation in the struggle to realize this utopia as the truest form of Christian worship. Thus, the EPIC movement as described in *Co-op* is promoted (as it often was during the historical EPIC campaign of 1934) by an ordained clergyman. The Self-Help Exchange's meeting takes place in the "assembly room" of the Grace Methodist Church, with the blessing of the church's minister, who prays for God's guidance in the new venture (53). Work for the cooperative movement is described as a form of "prayer" (389). Sinclair's narrator subsumes the commitment to a purely secular utopia under the heading of a "religious" undertaking. While the narrators of *After Many a Summer*, *The Day of the Locust*, *Parched Earth* and *The Grapes of Wrath* either critique or ignore Christianity, the narrator in *Co-op* seeks endorsement of the cooperative utopia by orthodox believers. He seeks to reassure them that the cooperative utopia represents not a negation, but a confirmation of their faith.

The prophet-figures' critique of historic and institutionalized religion is only one tactic, in a broader strategy of defamiliarizing established social conditions. They not only denounce what is, but announce what is to be, whether catastrophe, or new forms of community. Their authority in the latter respect is derived from parodic references to traditionally revered originals, and from the narrators' attribution to them of special insight into socio-cultural conditions.[39]

Whatever the nature of the prophet-figure's utopian message, the success of that message is inseparable from the setting in which it is preached. The rural/agricultural context is one in which partial acceptance of the prophet-figure's message may lead to a closer approximation of the present parodied to a more desirable one, in the sharing of the land's resources and in the literal or figurative restoration of women's capacity to nurture, as the prophet's message gains acceptance. In the artificial setting of the "natural museum," no utopia of community, mutuality or solidarity ever takes root. The organic metaphor is used advisedly. If the utopias of community only find acceptance in the context of the novels' rural/agricultural settings, there are obvious economic reasons why this development is, fictionally speaking, a plausible one. Beyond such practical considerations, though, one may detect other motivating factors. In Propter's nature mysticism, in Casy's organicist romanticism, in women's inability to bear and nurture outside of the rural/agricultural setting, one may detect an idealization of the setting for its own sake. A celebration of the pastoral, Eden/Canaan remains a more compelling model of utopia than the New Jerusalem—never to be realized, however, without the guidance of a prophet-figure, and human mutual cooperation.

Although the California Dream of individual fulfillment in isolation from a community, and in isolation from the land, is represented as illusory, aspirations to communally or cooperatively based prosperity are not. The "rich harvest" evoked at the close of *Parched Earth*, the repeated allusions to peaceful sharing of resources in *The Grapes of Wrath*, the hope of agricultural self-sufficiency in *After Many a Summer*, Sinclair's idyll of the cooperative in the little town among the hills in *Co-op*, all point beyond mere selfish individualism. Depression-era California, as gynaeceum and custodian of the Dream conceived of in terms of competitive individualism, also presents (at least potentially) a number of utopian alternatives. In the contemporary social context, the Depression-era novelists' representations of these alternatives as possible exclusively within the rural setting take on added resonance. In a period of widespread anxieties and uncertainties about the fate of those green expanses on which the very survival of our species depends, it may well be that the resonance has significance beyond the merely figurative.

Admittedly, the utopian potential of various communal or cooperative social visions, whether in fiction or in broader political contexts, has to the present day gone largely unheeded (and indeed such utopias are unfortunately currently conflated in many imaginations with totalitarianism). Yet who can tell? It is a potential to which, in another, perhaps not so remote time of crisis—as a socioeconomic order based on ever-expanding industrial production and the continuing exhaustion and destruction of the earth's resources comes to look increasingly impractical—interested sections of society may yet return.

Notes

1 Steinbeck was later to receive the assistance of Will Alexander, Deputy Administrator of the Federal Farm Security Administration, in his field research for *The Grapes of Wrath*. See Benson, "To Tom Who Lived It" 151-57.

2 And earlier at Dayton, Ohio, with the support of the Farm Resettlement Agency. See Robert Fogarty's introduction to *This Ugly Civilization*.

As George Woodcock has pointed out, Propter in *After Many a Summer* largely follows Borsodi's ideas on the development of the agrarian commune (222). Among those points on which he faithfully follows Borsodi are the significance Borsodi ascribes to the economic independence possible to the independent rural homestead, and the recognition that only a few "quality-minded" individuals, as Borsodi calls them, will ever choose such a way of life (*Civilization* 273, 319).

3 Heard also commends Borsodi's social theories and invokes him in defining his ideal for the self-sufficient religious community (*Pain* 221).

4 "Heard, in his new hypothesis of evolution, advocated the formation of small self-subsisting communities where techniques for psychological advancement could be explored in an atmosphere free from the distractions of civilization" (141).

5 A character in Huxley's later fiction does appear to think in terms akin to those of Heard, at least insofar as the evolution of human thought is concerned. "And now it's up to us to take another half turn up the spiral," Shanta in *Island* tells Will Farnaby. "Darwinism . . . was the old neolithic Wisdom turned into scientific concepts. The new conscious Wisdom . . . is biological theory realized in living practice, is Darwinism raised to the level of compassion and spiritual insight" (226).

6 Although Borsodi flatly rejects any notion of "the spiritual," and views the development of alternative communities as offering purely material benefits, this concept of marginal communities as an option for the few is basic to his thinking also (*Civilization* 428, 318).

7 Coutrot's social theories, partly developed through his experience as adviser to the Léon Blum cabinet during the factory occupations in France of 1936, are mainly concerned with economic and managerial reforms for the more efficient functioning of a centralized, industrialized society with a mixed economy. Coutrot argued for the establishment of cooperatives, workers' councils, the planned introduction of new technology, a welfare state and

"l'organization rationnelle et humaine de l'inégalité" (100-107). If Huxley's Propter owes anything to Coutrot, it may be the emphasis on the limitation of private wealth and on restrictions upon private ownership of the means of production (99-101). The debt, however, is clearly limited, compared with that which Propter owes to Borsodi and Heard.

8 For A.E. Dyson, writing in 1961, Huxley's pacifism had less to do with "any clear-cut social dynamic," than with "mysticism, the ultimate escape from committal. . . . And this, we cannot help remembering, is in 1935" (293). E.B. Burgum accused Huxley of adopting a "trance-like state of apathy" after his move to the United States. "The only domination Huxley fears," Burgum claimed, "is the one that might limit his own independence as an intellectual of the middle class" (141, 151). Such judgments risk overlooking Huxley's insistence that "Means determine ends." Huxley's resistance to the use of violence in politics, however impractical, is based on this principled assumption (See *Ends and Means* 28).

9 See Jerome Meckier, *Satire and Structure* 161. Keith May calls Propter's social philosophy "Jeffersonian democracy" (145). For Robert Baker, Propter's "Jeffersonian" sentiments conflict with his "puritanical" aversion to "all aspects of human experience" (192).

10 See *Letters* 362.

11 In *Ends and Means* (1937) Huxley suggested that, in a truly equitable society, the income of the lowest-paid individual should be no less than one-third of that of the highest paid (188).

12 Huxley writes, for instance, in 1932, with regard to the Scottsboro case, of the evils of any monopoly of the media: "It's terrifying what can be done by people who have a monopoly of the means of propaganda—private money—grubbers in the U.S.A., Musso and Co. in Italy, Communist Party in U.R.R.S." (361).

13 In the words of Chief Israel Satinpenny, "The day of vengeance is here. The star of the paleface is sinking and he knows it. Spengler has said so; Valéry has said so . . ." (233).

14 "London will burn . . . / The English worker will burn it / . . . The Negro will give him fire / Africa is the land of fire. . . . / London is tired / It will welcome the flame . . ." See Martin 331.

15 Like Eliot's London, West's Los Angeles is an "Unreal city," haunted by lost souls, whose inhabitants can "connect / Nothing with nothing." Its narrator, like the *persona* of *The Waste Land*, evokes—even invokes—the image of "Falling towers / Jerusalem Athens Alexandria . . ." (37-50).

16 "The prophets prophesy falsely, and the priests bear rule by their means; and my people love to have it so: and what will ye do in the end thereof?" (Jeremiah 5.31).

17 Socialist realism was essentially a conservative artistic trend, which denounced literary experimentation as "bourgeois formalism." What it retained from the Kharkov resolution was the dictum that literature should reveal the "decisive tendencies" of a historical movement towards socialism, believed to be inevitable. Socialist realism proved much less influential among North American leftist writers than Eastman had feared it would be.

18 In *The Radical Novel in the United States* (215-24).

19 A. Elistratova, writing in the first issue of the Comintern's literary journal, *International Literature*, in 1932, defined "prolit" as both Party-connected and working-class-oriented. She distinguished it from "revolutionary literature," which was not necessarily written by a Party member, but which offered a radical critique of society.

20 In fairness to the radical fiction of the 1930s, it should be said that it was more varied and less formulaic than is generally supposed, including as it did the lyrical prose of Josephine Herbst, the reportage of Meridel Le Sueur, the autobiographical writing of Mike Gold and the early short stories by Richard Wright. Even Armstrong's *Parched Earth*, whether judged to be "successful" as a work of fiction or not, is distinguished by its innovative use of figurative imagery. If the "proletarian novelists" were "artists in uniform," they were, as Rideout remarks, "a detachment of irregulars . . . decidedly fractious in discipline" (165).

21 "The Three Sources and Three Component Parts of Marxism." Tucker 640-44.

22 During his conflict with Saul, David gathered to him "everyone that was in distress, and everyone that was in debt, and everyone that was discontented," and became "a captain over them." They hid in the hills and the woods from the persecution of Saul (I Samuel 22.2, 29.19-24). This biblical incident suggests a possible further analogue between David and Dave Washburn, leader of the homeless cannery workers, whom he rallies in a camp in the woods.

23 The novel's principal capitalist is Caldwell, a "cold well," suggesting perhaps that the monopolized waters behind Everett Caldwell's dam are incapable of rendering the land fertile. A "burn" is a small stream; Washburn's healing waters, unlike Caldwell's, are capable of fertilizing the land.

24 Other influences on *The Grapes of Wrath* and its prophet-figure—Jeffersonian agrarianism, Transcendentalism, the anthropological theories of Briffault—have already been alluded to in earlier chapters of the present study. Moreover, the critical literature on these three influences in particular, is vast.

25 Hicks found in *The Grapes of Wrath* a convincing portrayal of the Joads as representative of a social class, but also "power, beauty and imagination" in narration (138-43). Six years earlier, taking V.F. Calverton to task for an allegedly over-simplistic judgment of radical literature, he had expressed

similar views, on the importance of a certain imaginative "intensity" in successful fiction; and added that a successful proletarian novel would "directly or indirectly" show "the effects of the class struggle" (11-12).

26 "Not only is it unthinkable that *The Grapes of Wrath* would have been enthusiastically received at the beginning of the thirties, but it is even unlikely that Steinbeck, who was not a 'proletarian novelist,' could have written the book without being aware of the efforts, crude or otherwise, made by the actual proletarians to solve the problems of ideological literature" (288).

27 Walter Fuller considered that Steinbeck expressed "hostility, bitterness, and contempt toward the middle classes." (See "The Grapes of Wrath Reconsidered" 136-44). In fact, Steinbeck *idealizes* one section of the middle class, that of the small entrepreneur.

28 "Regardless of his professed admiration for the 'Okies,' not for a moment does Steinbeck exempt the sharecroppers from their portion of blame for the ruined and impotent earth" (132). As Owens points out, the Okies, in their unthinking individualism, also express a "corrupt wish for a war to save them" from their economic plight through a rise in the price of cotton; and their individualistic ancestors have killed Indians and exhausted the land in their turn, before moving West: "The share-croppers of the Dust Bowl have failed in their responsibility to the land, and are sent on the road to learn a new commitment to one another and to the place they will eventually claim in a new land" (133).

29 Martin Shockley went so far as to argue that Casy is not merely a secular version of Christ, but that he is a "simple and direct copy of Jesus Christ" (87). However, the correspondence between Casy and Christ is not so obvious for all commentators; and the question of Tom's identity is treated as even more problematic. For Gerard Cannon—somewhat improbably, no doubt—Tom is Saint Paul, who at first rejected Christ's teaching, before himself becoming a convert (222). Charles Dougherty, on the other hand, sees Tom, not Casy, as the Christ-figure, on the grounds that "Tom is active and effective, while Casy is a dreamer" (224). For Thomas Dunn, Casy is Aaron, Tom is Moses—and Ma Joad is Deborah!

30 Sinclair later called his utopia "industrial democracy" (*Autobiography*).

31 See McIntosh 77-87. Broader public interest in the cooperative utopia is also suggested by demand for the EPIC program's newsletter, the *EPIC News*, which attained a circulation of nearly two million in its final two issues before the 1934 election (Harris 315).

32 It is perhaps not without significance that Sinclair's campaign manager, Richard Otto, was a former "Bellamyite," the founder of a Bellamy Society (*Autobiography* 269).

33 For the *persona* of *Le Spleen de Paris*, the city is "Hôpital, lupanar, purgatoire, enfer, bagne"—a vision not unlike that of Tod Hackett

("Epilogue" 310). Something of the character of Tod Hackett, physically clumsy and personally awkward, yet capable of poetic vision, may also be suggested by the poet of "L'Albatros" in *Les Fleurs du Mal.* The poet is likened to the albatross, "prince des nuées" who, grounded among mortals, finds his poetic gift only a hindrance: "Exilé sur le sol au milieu des huées, / Ses ailes de géant l'empêchent de marcher" (9-10).

34 Reid has suggested, for instance, that the character of Shrike in Miss Lonelyhearts may have been partly inspired by that of the diabolist Coleman in *Antic Hay*.

35 For Peter Firchow, Propter is "something of a gasbag . . . a passive, inactive preacher" (157). For Jerome Meckier, he is "more consistently boring" than earlier "mentor" figures in Huxley's fiction, such as Rampion in *Point Counter Point*—a character modeled on D.H. Lawrence (162).

36 Casy moves, as Peter Lisca suggests, "from Bible-belt evangelism to social prophecy" ("Fiction" 307).

37 In the words of Irving Malin, "As he learns, we learn" (85).

38 In *They Call Me Carpenter* (1922) Sinclair's narrator calls Jesus "the world's greatest revolutionary martyr, the founder of the world's first proletarian party" (224). His Christ-figure in this novel condemns exploitation and economic parasitism. His "Last Supper" takes place at the offices of the local chapter of the Socialist Party. In a pamphlet written for the EPIC campaign, Sinclair quotes his earlier statement from *The Profits of Religion*, on his hope of seeing the Christian ideal of "peace on earth and good will toward men" realized through socialism (*Lie Factory* 34). Sinclair's position on the relationship of Christianity to socialism seems to have remained essentially unchanged over four decades. In his autobiography of 1962, he writes of the sense of obligation of "truly religious people" to change "a world in which men exploit the labor of their fellows." In Sinclair's view, God dwells "in the hearts of human beings fighting for justice," even in those of social rebels, many of whom "reject his name" (283).

39 This is not to deny that each of the four texts studied here exhibits, to a varying degree, a "dialogic" texture, in the Bakhtinian sense of an interplay of voices and counter-voices which challenge the exclusive domination of the "monologic" narrator's voice. Indeed, as Bakhtin has pointed out, such dialogic tendencies are inevitably to be found in any text:

> The dialogic orientation of discourse is a phenomenon that is, of course, a property of any discourse. On all its various routes toward the object, in all its directions, the word encounters an alien word and cannot help encountering it in a living, tension-filled interaction. Only the mythical Adam, who approached a virginal and as yet verbally unqualified world with the first word, could really have escaped from start to finish this dialogic inter-orientation with the alien word that occurs in the object. ("Discourse in the Novel," Holquist 279.)

However, the texts of *Parched Earth*, *The Grapes of Wrath*, *After Many a Summer*, and *Co-op* to some extent "deviate," to use Bakhtin's own term, from this dialogic inter-orientation, through the powerful domination of character presentation and point of view by the voice of the author/narrator. The text of *The Day of the Locust*, on the other hand, is the locus of a number of clearly distinct and interacting parodic voices, in which one might speak of the narrator's "styles," rather than of a single, uniform "style" and univocal voice.

Bibliography

Allen, Walter. *The Modern Novel in Britain and the United States.* New York: E. P. Dutton, 1964.

Armstrong, Arnold B. *Parched Earth.* New York: Macmillan, 1934.

Astro, Richard. "From the Tidepool to the Stars: Steinbeck's Sense of Place." *Steinbeck Quarterly* 10.1 (1977): 5-11.

Auerback, Jerrold. *Labor and Liberty: The La Follette Committee and the New Deal.* New York and Indianapolis: Bobbs-Merrill, 1966.

Baker, Robert S. *The Dark Historic Page: Social Satire and Historicism in the Novels of Aldous Huxley, 1921-1939.* Madison: University of Wisconsin Press, 1982.

Baldanza, Frank. "Huxley and Hearst." *Journal of Modern Literature* 7.3 (1979): 441-55.

Balio, Tino, ed. *The American Film Industry.* Madison: University of Wisconsin Press, 1976.

Baudelaire, Charles. *Oeuvres Complètes.* Ed. Y-G. Le Dantec. Paris: Gallimard, 1961.

Bean, Walton. *California: An Interpretive History.* New York: McGraw-Hill, 1968.

Bedford, Sybille. *Aldous Huxley: A Biography.* New York: Harper and Row, 1969.

Bellamy, Edward. *Looking Backward, 2000-1887.* 1887. New York: New American Library, 1960.

Benson, Jackson J. "To Tom Who Lived It: John Steinbeck and the Man from Weedpatch." *Journal of Modern Literature* 15 (1979): 151-97.

______. *The True Adventures of John Steinbeck, Writer.* New York: Viking Press, 1984.

Bloom, Harold, ed. *John Steinbeck.* New York: Chelsea House Publishers, 1987.

______. *Nathanael West.* New York: Chelsea House Publishers, 1986.

Bogardus, Ralph F. and Hobson, Fred C., eds. *Literature at the Barricades: The American Writer in the 1930s.* Alabama: University of Alabama Press, 1982.

Borsodi, Ralph. *This Ugly Civilization.* 1929. Philadelphia: Porcupine Press, 1975.

Bowden, James H. "No Redactor, No Reward." Madden, 283-97.

Bowering, Peter. *Aldous Huxley: A Study of the Major Novels.* London: Athlone Press, 1968.

Bowron, Bernard. "*The Grapes of Wrath*: A 'Wagons West' Romance." *Colorado Quarterly* 3 (Summer 1954): 84-91.

Briffault, Robert. *The Mothers: The Matriarchal Theory of Social Origins.* New York: Macmillan, 1931.

Brown, Norman O. *Life Against Death: The Psychoanalytical Meaning of History.* Middletown, Connecticut: Wesleyan University Press, 1959.

Burgum, Edwin B. *The Novel and the World's Dilemma.* New York: Oxford University Press, 1947.

Burke, Fielding. *Call Home the Heart.* 1932. New York: The Feminist Press, 1983.

Burke, Robert E. *Olson's New Deal for California*. Berkeley and Los Angeles: University of California Press, 1953.

Cannon, Gerard. "The Pauline Apostleship of Tom Joad." *College English* 24.3 (1962): 222-24.

Cantwell, Robert. *The Land of Plenty*. New York: Farrar and Rinehart, 1934.

Carpenter, Frederic C. "The Philosophical Joads." *College English* 2 (January 1941): 315-25.

Caughey, John W. *California: A Remarkable State's Life History*. New Jersey: Prentice-Hall, 1970.

Chambers, Clarke A. *California Farm Organizations: A Historical Study of the Grange, the Farm Bureau and the Associated Farmers, 1929-1941*. Berkeley: University of California Press, 1952.

Cleland, Robert Glass. *From Wilderness to Empire*. New York: Knopf, 1962.

Coutrot, Jean. *L'Humanisme Economique*. Paris: Centre polytechnicien d'études, 1936.

Covici, Pascal, ed. *The Portable Steinbeck*. New York: Viking, 1943.

Crockett, H. Kelly. "The Bible and *The Grapes of Wrath*." *College English* 24.3 (1962): 193-99.

Dardis, Tom. *Some Time in the Sun*. 1976. Harmondsworth: Penguin, 1981.

Ditsky, John. "*The Grapes of Wrath*: A Reconsideration." *Southern Humanities Review* 13.3 (1979): 215.

Dougherty, Charles T. "The Christ-Figure in *The Grapes of Wrath*." *College English* 24.3 (1962): 224-26.

Dunn, Thomas F. "*The Grapes of Wrath.*" *College English* 24.7 (1963): 566-67.

Dyson, A. E. "Aldous Huxley and the Two Nothings." *Critical Quarterly* 3 (1961): 293-309.

Eagleton, Terry. *Criticism and Ideology: A Study in Marxist Literary Theory.* 1975. London: Verso Editions, 1980.

Eastman, Max. "Artists in Uniform." *Modern Monthly* 7.7 (August) 1933: 397-404.

Eisinger, Chester. "Jeffersonian Agrarianism in *The Grapes of Wrath.*" *University of Kansas City Review* 14 (Winter) 1947: 149-54.

Eliot, T. S. *The Complete Poems and Plays, 1909-1950.* New York: Harcourt, Brace and World, 1971.

Elistratova, A. "*New Masses.*" *International Literature* 1 (1932): 107-11.

Falkenberg, Sandra. "A Study of Female Characterization in Steinbeck's Fiction." *Steinbeck Quarterly* 8.2 (1975): 50-55.

Firchow, Peter. *Aldous Huxley: Satirist and Novelist.* Minnesota: University of Minnesota Press, 1972.

Fitzgerald, F. Scott. *The Last Tycoon.* New York: Scribners, 1941.

Folsom, Michael, ed. *Mike Gold: A Literary Anthology.* New York: International Publishers, 1972.

Fontenrose, Joseph. *John Steinbeck: An Introduction and Interpretation.* New York: Barnes and Noble, 1963.

Fossey, W. Richard. "The End of the Western Dream: *The Grapes of Wrath* and Oklahoma." *Cimarron Review* 22 (1973): 25-34.

French, Warren, ed. *A Companion to The Grapes of Wrath.* New York: Viking, 1963.

______. *John Steinbeck.* New York: Twayne, 1961.

Fuller, Walter I. "*The Grapes of Wrath* Reconsidered." *Mississippi Quarterly* 12 (Summer) 1959: 136-44.

Gold, Michael. "Proletarian Realism." *New Masses* 6 (September) 1930: 3-5.

"*The Grapes of Wrath.*" *Collier's* 104 (September 2): 1934: 54.

Greenway, John. *American Folksongs of Protest.* New York: Octagon, 1977.

Guthrie, Woody. "Do Re Mi." TRO copyright, 1961. New York: Ludlow Music, 1963.

Harris, Leon. *Upton Sinclair: American Rebel.* New York: Thomas Crowell, 1975.

Heard, Gerald. *Pain, Sex and Time: A New Outlook on Evolution and the Future of Man.* New York and London: Harper and Brothers, 1939.

______. "The Poignant Prophet." *Kenyon Review* 27 (1965): 49-70.

Herbst, Josephine. "Nathanael West." *Kenyon Review* 23 (1961): 611-30.

Hine, Robert V. *California's Utopian Colonies.* San Marino: Huntington Library, 1953.

Holquist, Michael, ed. *The Dialogic Imagination: Four Essays by M. M. Bakhtin.* Austin: University of Texas Press, 1981.

Huxley, Aldous. *After Many a Summer Dies the Swan.* London: Chatto and Windus, 1939.

______. *Antic Hay*. New York: Harper and Brothers, 1923.

______. *Those Barren Leaves*. 1925. Harmondsworth: Penguin, 1955.

______. *Ends and Means: An Inquiry into the Nature of Ideals and into the Methods employed for their Realization*. London: Chatto and Windus, 1937.

______. *Eyeless in Gaza*. London: Chatto and Windus, 1936.

______. *Island*. London: Chatto and Windus, 1962.

Joyce, James. *Ulysses*. 1922. New York: Random House, 1986.

Kasson, John. *Civilizing the Machine: Technology and Republican Values in America, 1776-1900*. Harmondsworth: Penguin, 1977.

Kolodny, Annette. *The Lay of the Land*. Chapel Hill: University of North Carolina Press, 1975.

Lenin, V. I. *One Step Forward, Two Steps Back*. In *Collected Works* 7. Ed. Clemens Dutt. Moscow: Foreign Languages Publishing House, 1961.

Levant, Howard. *The Novels of John Steinbeck: A Critical Study*. Columbia: University of Missouri Press, 1974.

Lewis, R. W. B. *The American Adam*. Chicago: University of Chicago Press, 1955.

Light, James F. *Nathanael West: An Interpretative Study*. Evanston: Northwestern University Press, 1971.

______. "Nathanael West and the Ravaging Locust." *American Quarterly* 12 (Spring) 1960: 44-54.

Lisca, Peter. "*The Grapes of Wrath* as Fiction." *PMLA* 72 (March) 1957: 296-309.

Lokke, V. L. "A Side Glance at Medusa: Hollywood, the Literature Boys and Nathanael West." *Southwest Review* 46 (1961): 35-45.

Madden, David, ed. *Nathanael West: The Cheaters and the Cheated. A Collection of Critical Essays.* Deland, Florida: Everett/Edwards, 1973.

Malin, Irving. *Nathanael West's Novels.* Carbondale: Southern Illinois University Press, 1972.

Mannheim, Karl. *Ideology and Utopia.* New York: Harcourt, Brace, Jovanovitch, 1955.

Martin, Jay. *Nathanael West: The Art of His Life.* New York: Farrar Straus and Giroux, 1970.

______, ed. *Nathanael West: A Collection of Critical Essays.* Englewood Cliffs, New Jersey: Prentice-Hall, 1971.

Martin, Stoddard. *California Writers.* New York: St. Martin's Press, 1983.

Marx, Karl. *Capital, vol. 1.* New York: Vintage Press, 1976.

Marx, Leo. *The Machine in the Garden: Technology and the Pastoral Ideal in America.* New York: Oxford University Press, 1964.

May, Keith. *Aldous Huxley.* New York: Harper and Row, 1972.

McIntosh, Clarence Fredric. "Upton Sinclair and the EPIC Movement, 1933-1936." (Unpublished doctoral dissertation.) Stanford: Stanford University, 1974.

McWilliams, Carey. "California Party Lines All Snarled." *Baltimore Sun* 7 October, 1934: 1-2.

______. *The Education of Carey McWilliams.* New York: Simon and Schuster, 1978.

_____. *Factories in the Field: The Story of Migratory Farm Labor in California*. Boston: Little, Brown and Co., 1939.

_____. "Reactions for Merriam Seen, but Observer Holds G.O.P. Tactics May Bring Defeat." *Baltimore Sun* 21 October, 1934: 1, 21.

_____. "Sunlight in My Soul." *The Aspirin Age*. Ed. Isabel Leighton. New York: Simon and Schuster, 1949.

Meckier, Jerome. *Aldous Huxley: Satire and Structure*. London: Chatto and Windus, 1969.

Miron, George Thomas. *The Truth About John Steinbeck and the Migrants*. Los Angeles: Haynes Corporation, 1939.

Mitchell, Ruth Comfort. *Of Human Kindness*. New York: Appleton-Century, 1940.

Motley, Warren. "From Patriarchy to Matriarchy: Ma Joad's Role in *The Grapes of Wrath*." *American Literature* 54.3 (1982): 397-412.

NANA, Inc. "Dust Bowl Exiles Roam California." *New York Times* 18 July, 1937, sec. 2:1.

Nebberger, Richard. "Who Are the Associated Farmers?" *Survey Graphic* 28 (1939): 518-20, 555-57.

Neufeldt, Leonard. *The Economist: Henry Thoreau and Enterprise*. New York: Oxford University Press, 1989.

Norris, Frank. *The Octopus: A Story of California*. New York: Doubleday and Page and Co., 1903.

Owens, Louis. *John Steinbeck's Re-vision of America*. Athens: University of Georgia Press, 1985.

Piper, Henry Dan, ed. *Think Back on Us: A Contemporary Chronicle of the 1930s*. Carbondale: Southern Illinois University Press, 1967.

Reid, Randall. *The Fiction of Nathanael West: No Redeemer, No Promised Land*. Chicago and London: University of Chicago Press, 1967.

Rideout, Walter B. *The Radical Novel in the United States, 1900-1954: Some Interrelations of Literature and Society*. Cambridge: Harvard University Press, 1965.

Robbins, Jack Alan, ed. *Granville Hicks in The New Masses*. New York: The Kennikat Press, 1974.

Rolle, Andrew. *California: A History*. New York: Crowell, 1969.

Roske, Ralph J. *Everyman's Eden: A History of California*. New York: Macmillan, 1968.

Rosten, Leo C. *Hollywood: The Movie Colony, the Movie Makers*. New York: Harcourt, Brace and Co., 1941.

Sanford, Charles L. "Classics of American Reform Literature." *American Quarterly* 10 (Fall) 1958: 295-311.

Schulberg, Budd. *What Makes Sammy Run?* New York: Random House, 1941.

______. "Writers in America." *The Four Seasons of Success*. New York: Stein and Day, 1983.

Seaver, Edwin. "Revolution by Water." *New Republic* 25 April, 1934: 315.

Shockley, Martin. "Christian Symbolism in *The Grapes of Wrath*." *College English* 18.2 (1956): 87-90.

Sinclair, Upton B. *The Autobiography of Upton Sinclair.* New York: Harcourt, Brace and World, 1962.

______. *Co-op: A Novel of Living Together.* 1936. London: T. Werner Laurie, 1948.

______. *I, Governor of California and How I Ended Poverty in California: A True Story of the Future.* Los Angeles: Upton Sinclair, 1933.

______. *The Lie Factory Starts.* Los Angeles: End Poverty League, Inc., 1934.

______. *They Call Me Carpenter: A Tale of the Second Coming.* Pasadena, California: Upton Sinclair, 1922.

Smith, Grover, ed. *Letters of Aldous Huxley.* London: Chatto and Windus, 1969.

Smith, Henry Nash. *Virgin Land: The American West as Symbol and Myth.* New York: Random House, 1950.

Spengler, Oswald. *The Decline of the West.* 1926-1928. New York: A. A. Knopf, 1939.

Spivak, Gayatri Chakravorty. *In Other Worlds: Essays in Cultural Politics.* London: Methuen, 1987.

Starr, Kevin. *Inventing the Dream: California Through the Progressive Era.* New York: Oxford University Press, 1985.

Stein, Walter J. *California and the Dust Bowl Migrants.* Westport, Connecticut: Greenwood Press, 1973.

Steinbeck, Elaine, and Wallsten, Robert, eds. *John Steinbeck: A Life in Letters.* London: Heinemann, 1975.

Steinbeck, John. *The Grapes of Wrath.* 1939. Harmondsworth: Penguin, 1977.

_____. *In Dubious Battle*. New York: Modern Library, 1936.

_____. *The Long Valley*. 1938. New York: Viking, 1956.

Swanberg, W. A. *Citizen Hearst: A Biography of William Randolph Hearst*. New York: Charles Scribner's Sons, 1961.

Todd, Charles L. "The 'Okies' Search for a Lost Frontier." *New York Times Magazine*, 27 August 1939: 11.

Trachtenberg, Stanley. "John Steinbeck: The Fate of Protest." *North Dakota Quarterly* 41.2 (1973): 5-11.

_____. "West's Locusts: Laughing at the Laugh." *Michigan Quarterly Review* 14 (1975): 187-98.

Tucker, Robert C., ed. *The Lenin Anthology*. New York: Norton, 1975.

Vorse, Mary Heaton. *Strike!* New York: Horace Liveright, 1930.

Wadlington, Warwick. "Nathanael West and the Confidence Game." Madden, 299-322.

Wells, Walter. "Shriek of the Locusts." *Tycoons and Locusts: A Regional Look at Hollywood Fiction of the 1930s*. Carbondale and Edwardsville: Southern Illinois University Press, 1973: 49-70.

West, Nathanael. *A Cool Million*. 1934. *Complete Works*, Ed. Alan Ross. New York: Farrar, Straus and Cudahy, 1957.

_____. *The Day of the Locust*. 1939. New York: New Directions, 1962.

_____. *Miss Lonelyhearts*. 1933. New York: New Directions, 1962.

"Whither the American Writer (A Questionnaire)." *Modern Quarterly* 6.2 (Summer) 1932: 11-20.

"Who Are the Associated Farmers?" *The Associated Farmer* 15 April 1940: 3-4.

Wilson, Edmund. *The American Earthquake: A Documentary of the Twenties and Thirties*. New York: Farrar Straus and Giroux, 1975.

______. "The Boys in the Back Room." *Classics and Commercials: A Literary Chronicle of the Forties*. New York: Farrar, Straus and Giroux, 1950.

Wolfe, Thomas Kennerly, Jr. "The League of American Writers: Communist Organizational Activity Among American Writers, 1929-1942." (Unpublished doctoral dissertation.) New Haven, Connecticut: Yale University, 1956.

Woodcock, George. *Dawn and the Darkest Hour: A Study of Aldous Huxley*. New York: Viking, 1972.

Wright, Celeste Turner. "Ancient Analogues of an Incident in John Steinbeck." *Western Folklore* 14 (1955): 50-51.

Wyatt, David. *The Fall into Eden: Landscape and Imagination in California*. Cambridge: Cambridge University Press, 1986.

Index